BINGE THINKING

BINGE THINKING

A Different Kind of College Hangover

Zachary M. White, Ph.D.
and
Gino D. Borges, Ph.D.

iUniverse, Inc.
New York Lincoln Shanghai

Binge Thinking
A Different Kind of College Hangover

iUniverse books may be ordered through booksellers or by contacting:

iUniverse
2021 Pine Lake Road, Suite 100
Lincoln, NE 68512
www.iuniverse.com
1-800-Authors (1-800-288-4677)

ISBN-13: 978-0-595-34761-2 (pbk)
ISBN-13: 978-0-595-79503-1 (ebk)
ISBN-10: 0-595-34761-4 (pbk)
ISBN-10: 0-595-79503-X (ebk)

Printed in the United States of America

Dear Helpers,

What a thankless job you didn't sign up for. Don, Jason, Angie, Paul, Dr. Will, Holly, Mike, Robin, Geoff, Nan, Steve, Chris, and Sarah, you deserve so much more recognition than this mere acknowledgment page. To reconcile this transgression, a cameo character that symbolized your talents and kindness was originally considered for *Binge Thinking*. But after numerous meetings with our in-house literary agent (us), we were advised to drop your cameo character on the grounds that accepting you meant rejecting somebody else. Blame DB! It's because of your insightful comments and invaluable edits that our private neuroses became clear enough for others to laugh at, enjoy, and learn from.

We'd also like to thank our families who stuck with us as we pursued this book in spite of countless obstacles. We're forever grateful that you never once questioned the merits of this book—just our sanity.

Finally, we're indebted to the professors, administrators, counselors, peers, and students who provided perpetual inspiration for our bouts of binge thinking and ultimately for this book. We couldn't have nor would we have wanted to write this book without your most unusual contributions.

In care,

Zachary and Gino

The Binge Thinking Menu

The Untold Story of Binge Thinking 1

Tortured by the "Too" Tyler 6

Moment Abuser Maya 25

Addicted to Aloneness Anna 49

Belongaholic Beck 72

Potentializer Paula 87

Students Who Binge Together, Stay Together 107

Dear College Students 127

Dear Parents of College Students 128

Dear Colleges and Universities 129

About Borges and White, LLC 131

The Untold Story of Binge Thinking

"You know what binge drinking is—
from what others tell you, of course—
but binge thinking is a kind of college excess that you can't avoid
no matter how hard you try."

Everywhere we turned, family, friends, high school counselors and teachers, college professors, and even complete strangers told us time and time again that college would be the best time of our lives. These kind-hearted people told us little else about the college experience other than that it was the best time of their lives. After all we heard, we couldn't help but buy into the hype and expect our everyday college existence to look and feel as advertised.

What we didn't know, unfortunately, was that we would indulge in binge thinking while in college. Although Gino and I attended different schools, we both binged on thoughts of loneliness even when surrounded by people seemingly like ourselves. We binged on ways to distinguish ourselves as successful beyond the measure of grades, even though we earned good grades. We binged on our desires to find where and with whom we most belonged, even as we participated in campus clubs and organizations. We binged on our attempts to find the perfect relationship, even when we were dating someone at the time. We binged on our feelings of dissatisfaction when everyone around us seemed to be having a better time than we were. Finally, we binged on our fears of finding the perfect job and planning for a future we were told would bring us happiness, even though much of the time, we felt lost and aimless. While on our individual journeys through college, Zachary and I privately asked ourselves if there was something wrong with us or if someone forgot to tell us the full story of what really happens during that time between college admission and graduation.

Gino and I eventually crossed paths while receiving our Ph.D.s. As teachers, we heard stories of frustration, disappointment, and confusion from freshmen and seniors, liberal arts and science majors, from students preparing for graduate school and students who had perfected the art of just getting by. Class after class, semester after semester, and year after year, we had the opportunity to listen to our students' stories about their college encounters. While all of our students were warned of the highly-publicized behavioral risks of the college experience—unprotected sex, STDs, illicit drugs, smoking, under- and overeating, drinking and driving, and binge drinking—they weren't prepared to handle the less-publicized yet equally dangerous college phenomenon we call "binge thinking."

After years of research as students, graduate students, and professors, Zachary and I discovered that *all* college students binge think on one or more of the following:

- The stress of dissatisfaction
- The desire for recognition
- Thoughts of loneliness
- The need to belong
- Finding a perfect relationship and an ideal job

The good news is that these binges aren't entirely your fault. You weren't adequately prepared to overcome these universal, but overlooked, excesses of thought inherent in the college experience.

You know what binge drinking is—from what others tell you, of course—but binge thinking is a kind of college excess that you can't avoid no matter how hard you try. When you binge think, the excesses are of your mind and not of your body. Your body has a breaking point when it comes to physical excess: you know when you've gone too far. Your body won't let you forget! Binge thinking, unlike binge drinking and other forms of physical excess, can be harmful because it's so hard to know *when* you're binging.

Binge thinking is difficult to diagnose and treat because you can't simply change your behavior to prevent binge thinking like you can by saying "NO!" to unprotected sex, illicit drugs, smoking, under- and overeating, drinking and driving, and binge drinking. Sometime during college, you will indulge in an institutionally-approved way of thinking without fully understanding how the very excesses of thought necessary to help you win praise and attention in college—good grades, active social life, rewarding relationships, community involvement, leadership positions, and securing the ideal job after graduation—also shape who you are, what you think about, and what you do and don't do. As you, your parents, and your creditors know, no one wants to drop serious coin for an unfulfilling college experience. What you need is a way to meaningfully understand and talk about the real-life mental challenges you face in and out of the classroom.

Gino and I developed a "binge" vocabulary to help our students— and ourselves, since we aren't completely altruistic—understand how the institutionally-approved patterns of thought in college shaped and determined our students' private thoughts and feelings. When our students had a way to talk about binge thinking, they were able to separate themselves from their binges. With a binge vocabulary, they were able to question their thoughts rather than doubt their sanity and punish themselves with questions such as these: Why am I not always having the time of my life? Why are others having the best time of their lives and I'm not? Why am I different? Why do I feel alone even though I'm surrounded by so many people like me? Why are my spring breaks not like the ones I see on MTV? Sorry, that last question is one that Zachary still asks himself to this day.

With binge terms for their real-life binges, our students were able to realize something we wish we had known when we were undergraduates: they weren't the only ones who occasionally questioned themselves during the so-called best time of their lives. Word quickly spread about our ideas, and students began lining up outside our offices. In the midst of our first brush with popularity, students, student-life personnel, and even parents encouraged us to put our ideas into a book to make our insights publicly available.

Binge Thinking is a conversation-driven series of parables based on our experiences with binge thinking and our research on student life as graduate students and professors. It looks and sounds nothing like a textbook. We must admit, however, that this book should be listed on every syllabus as required reading since it spells out the very situations that conflict you in and out of the classroom. *Binge Thinking* is unlike most of the books you'll read in college because it doesn't contain the tools of precision you're so familiar with—statistics, graphs, or pie charts. The college truths in *Binge Thinking* can't be neatly summarized in easy-to-find bullet points—they can only be understood in the process of conversation. You should know that agents and publishers encouraged us to flex our academic muscle by writing a book that showcased our institutional credentials. That book would have contained countless statistics and trivial citations from arcane academic journals: the very features that scream boredom and taste like required reading. While their suggestions were sincere, we knew that if we wrote the book they preferred, you would have written us off as boring (side note to readers: we would have written ourselves off as boring as well).

You will, however, recognize the thinking binges of the five fictional students found on the campus of Shadow University. In *Binge Thinking*, you won't learn much about the characters beyond the essential features of their binges. These characters represent worst-case binge thinking scenarios; they may appear intense and even pitiful. They were partly inspired by our binge thinking; and yes, that means as undergraduates, we binged too. In the darkest and most harrowing moments of these students' struggles with binge thinking, a character named DB appears. DB diagnoses and cures each student's particular binge. DB's insights represent everything we've learned about how to diagnose and cure the inevitable and inescapable bouts of binge thinking. We wish DB could have helped us when we were undergraduates.

Tortured by the "Too" Tyler

"One day I don't have enough of something, the next day I have it,
and as soon as I get it, I feel like I have too much and want to get rid of
it again. Or, one day I have too much of something,
the next day I get rid of it, and then all of a sudden, I miss it!"

Tyler was excited about the prospect of living the dream of the college experience so many talked about. Before he left for school, everyone had advice for him. All of the advice he received, however, came in the form of warnings that, when taken to heart, were contradictory.

Tyler's parents warned him that while in college, he would constantly have to say "no" to unprotected sex, illicit drugs, binge drinking, drinking and driving, and the evil and ever-present influence of peer pressure. They said, out of care and concern, "Tyler, college is the opportunity for you to make something out of your life. It's a wonderful time, but be careful—some people don't take advantage of this great opportunity. It takes advantage of them."

Tyler's high school teachers warned him that while in college, there would be an increased need to study. They said, out of care and concern, "Tyler, you've done well in high school, but wait until you get into college—you're going to have to study twice as hard just to get the grades you're used to getting."

Tyler's older friends warned him that while in college, he shouldn't squander any opportunities to live life to the fullest. They said, out of care and concern, "Tyler, you don't want to miss out on all the opportunities for fun—drinking, dating, partying. This is the time of your life! You're supposed to let loose, so don't be too serious. Don't limit yourself! There will be plenty of time for falling in love and all that kind of stuff after you graduate."

Tyler's high school counselor warned him that while in college, there would be an excessive amount of free time. His counselor said, out of care and concern, "Tyler, you'll only be in class 15 hours a week. What's going to make you stand out in college is what you do with the time you aren't in class. Be careful about falling into the trap of becoming lazy. Make something of yourself."

Even the Shadow U president talked about the prospects of the college experience. During orientation week, the entire freshman class was packed into the basketball arena. As the new faces anxiously prepared themselves for the excesses they had been warned about and eagerly anticipated, the Shadow U president addressed them:

> Your college experience is a once-in-a-lifetime experience. From this day forward, you have the opportunity to determine the course of your life. The choices you make and the choices you don't make will make you. All of you are adults now, and here at Shadow U, you'll find that your choices will form the foundation of your character. The choices you make at Shadow U will forever be a part of your social DNA—you'll be a product of whom you spend time with, what subjects you decide to dedicate all-night study sessions to, the activities and groups you participate in, and the people you date and with whom you fall in love. There are many challenges ahead for all of you. But, remember above all else: don't let a minute go by without fully embracing this experience. Your parents, your friends, and even our culture are envious of the opportunities before you. Everyone wishes they could relive their own college experience.

Their time has passed; your time is now. Carpe diem! Seize the day! Don't let one moment pass in which you might regret what you did or didn't do on this beautiful campus amidst this wonderful opportunity: your college experience.

Tyler was finally at the doorstep of secular heaven. All possibilities were before him. One thing was for sure: Tyler was going to take the advice of everyone who'd taken the time to prepare him for this great experience.

*   *   *

Toward the end of his freshman year, Tyler found himself telling his parents about how bored he had become talking about the same old things with his friends and watching reruns of *The Real World* with the guys in the dorm. At first, he recalled, it was fun and exciting. He got to meet new people, and they were doing the same. It was bonding at its best. As the weeks progressed, however, what had seemed so new and exciting became routine and unsatisfying.

The boredom that marked the final weeks of his freshman year got worse over the summer. He couldn't get a job while living at home, so he spent most of his summer watching television, reading magazines, and getting a tan. He spent some time with old friends from high school, but most of them were off doing other things. Tyler was more than bored. He was frustrated. He couldn't get over the fact that something was missing. "No one told me about their memories of boredom and depression when they talked about their college experiences," he thought to himself while sitting by the pool, alone.

According to what everyone had told him, he wasn't supposed to be bored. While at home, his parents asked him why he was so unhappy. "I have too much time on my hands," he told them.

"Things are going to have to change," he resolved to himself.

When Tyler arrived at Shadow U for the beginning of a new school year, his sophomore year, things did change.

     *   *   *

Tyler typically called his parents on Sundays after dinner to let them know what he was doing and how he was feeling and sometimes, just to hear familiar voices. It was an essential part of his weekly routine.

"Hi Mom, hey Dad," Tyler said to his parents the second week of classes his sophomore year. His parents often got on the telephone at the same time to begin the phone conversation, and then, eventually, his dad would get off the phone, and his mom would continue talking. Tyler loved the setup. He felt comfortable saying some things to both his parents, and some things he felt more comfortable saying to his mother.

"Hello, Tyler," they responded in unison. "How are things going?" his mother asked.

"Great."

"Have you been able to get more involved like you said you wanted to?" his dad asked him with genuine care and interest.

"Actually, I have! It's unbelievable. Everything is falling into place all at once. In addition to the eighteen units I'm taking this semester, I'm also a volunteer counselor for troubled teens. Plus, I'm a tutor for a local junior high. And, to top it all off—and this is the best part—I was chosen by my favorite math professor to be a teaching assistant for one of his classes!"

"Wow," they responded in unison. "Congratulations, Tyler!" his mom said. "We're so proud of you. You're making the changes you talked about in the summer—definitely something to be proud of!"

Unlike during his freshman year, Tyler busied himself around the clock. He was finally going to experience all the opportunities his friends, family, and even the president of Shadow U had told him about.

A month later, as Sunday evening approached, Tyler wasn't sure he was going to have time to call his parents. Everything was catching up

with him. His eighteen units required more work than he had anticipated, and the helpline for teens required fifteen hours a week, not
including all the training hours he had to put in since he was new. He
also had to drive thirty minutes two times a week to the junior high
where he volunteered; and finally, to add to his already overwhelming
schedule, the professor he assisted had him grading exams nonstop!

Rushed and ragged, Tyler made it back to his dorm later than usual.
He called his parents.

"Hey Mom, hi Dad."

"Hey Honey, hi Son," they responded.

"Sorry for calling a bit late tonight."

"No problem, Tyler." His dad could tell he was busy by the rushed
tone in his weary voice. "How are things going?"

"I can't believe how much I've been doing the last month. I'm so
busy. I'm totally stressed out. I keep getting headaches and my stomach
is in knots. I can't get to sleep until 2 a.m., and I have to get up at 6:30
a.m. to try and fit everything in. Sometimes, I don't even have time for
lunch. You know how much I hate missing meals. It's really getting to
me. I don't have any time to spend with friends anymore. The last time
I went out for fun seems like, well, I can't even remember the last time I
went out without worrying about what I had to do the next morning."

His mother responded with concern: "Tyler, do you think you're
doing too much? Remember, there's only so much of you to go around."

"I'm just working too hard. I'm doing too many things for too many
people. I don't have any time to do the things I really want to do anymore."

Less than a year ago, Tyler had been bored because he didn't have
enough to do. Now Tyler was stressed out because he had too much to
do and no time to spend doing the things he really wanted to.

*　　　　　*　　　　　*

In the midst of all his activities, he met Janel, a fellow Shadow U student, while working at the teen helpline. They joked around while working. She laughed at his cheesy jokes. They were good for each other because they gave each other reason to laugh in otherwise stressful volunteer positions.

Tyler and Janel started to hang out after work. At first, it was once or twice a week. He helped her with calculus; she helped him with English. After a month, Tyler and Janel were joined at the hip, seeing each other as much as possible, even though both of them had hectic schedules. On the days they didn't see each other, they called each other several times a day just to say "hello" so they could hear each other's voices.

Tyler became so consumed with Janel that he didn't think about much else. One Sunday evening, while lying on his bed, dreaming about what he might get Janel for her birthday, his cell phone rang. Startled out of his dream state, Tyler answered his phone.

"Hello, Tyler," his dad said.

"Hello. Oh yeah, it's Sunday night. I totally forgot. I'm sorry. How are you two doing?"

"We're doing well," his father said. "How are things for you? We haven't heard from you much lately. Have you been able to get a little time for yourself?"

"Things are going much better. I was a bit overwhelmed with everything I was doing so I asked the math professor to reduce my grading workload. I also decided to drop a class I can take next semester, so I'm down to fifteen units instead of eighteen. I'm still overwhelmed, but things are better."

"You're only human, Tyler," his mom added. "I was worried about how much you were doing."

"There's also something else. I met this girl. Her name is Janel."

Though a bit startled, they both were happy for their son. Tyler's mom was intrigued about his new relationship. She asked, "What's she like?"

"When we have time, we eat together at the cafeteria; she comes over to my dorm to study; and on the weekends, we go to a restaurant to grab something nice to eat. She also likes a lot of the same things I do."

"So what's she like?" Tyler's mom asked again, wanting to know some specifics about Tyler and Janel's relationship.

"Well, we just have fun together no matter what we're doing. She appreciates the little things in life."

"Little things?" his mother asked curiously.

"She text-messages me throughout the day and tells me that she misses me and can't wait to see me. Better yet, whenever I have a test, she drops by my place to wish me luck. It's great. I never thought I would appreciate that stuff; but the more she does it, the more I know she's different from the other girls I've dated."

"We're excited for you," his dad declared.

"I gotta go. Janel is coming over and I need to clean up before she gets here. Talk to you soon," Tyler said with a laugh, as he ended the phone call.

After dating for a month, Tyler and Janel spent every precious free minute together. When weekends rolled around, it was assumed they would spend as much time together as they could. They didn't even ask each other anymore.

*   *

Two months into Tyler's relationship with Janel, Tyler's parents noticed a marked change in his voice from the previous weeks they'd talked on the phone.

Tyler's mom asked, "How's Janel doing?" Tyler paused before answering. He then said, "Oh, she's fine. What about you two?"

"Are you sure everything is okay, son?" Tyler's dad asked, not wanting to pry, but curious about the changes in his demeanor from only several weeks ago when he had been unable to stop talking about Janel.

"Yeah, I think so. Hey, how do you know when you're spending too much time with someone?"

Tyler's parents knew immediately that this wasn't a hypothetical question. Being the good parents they were, they didn't provide an answer, just another question to get Tyler to expand on what was really bothering him. "What do you mean?" his dad asked.

"I really care about Janel, but I feel like I don't have my own time anymore. I love doing stuff with her, calling her, going out with her on the weekends—but I'm in college. Shouldn't I date other people? I guess what I'm saying is that I feel smothered—I need more of my own space. I need to be more of my own person," Tyler said with confidence, as if he had practiced his response in advance.

After thinking all week about his relationship with Janel, he finally decided to tell her what was on his mind. He told her how much he cared for her, but because they both were in college, it wasn't right that they spent so much time together. Tyler told Janel, "I really care about you, but I need my own space. I think we've been spending too much time together. I want you to be able to be your own person, too. You understand, don't you? I don't know if you've noticed, but I've neglected everything else in my life—my classes, my friends, and all of my other commitments."

Janel didn't understand. "Too much time together?" she said to herself after Tyler walked away. "That doesn't make any sense. I don't understand. Aren't you supposed to spend a lot of time together with someone you care about?"

Tyler's mind was made up. He knew he cared for Janel, yet his care for her didn't outweigh his need for space. Independence overshadowed care. So Tyler set sail to rediscover who he was without Janel. Her presence was too much to manage in light of his desire for independence.

"So you broke up with Janel?" his mom asked in disbelief, after Tyler recounted his encounter with Janel earlier that week.

"Yeah, it's for the best," Tyler said. "I devoted too much time to her. Not only time, but too much money, too many thoughts. I finally came to the conclusion that Janel was cramping my style. I didn't have any energy or desire for anything else. That can't be healthy, right? I shouldn't settle down while I'm in college, right? I haven't spent enough time dating other girls. How do I know if she's right for me? Anyway, we're still going to be friends. So, not much is going to change."

Tyler's questions seemed more like answers, so his parents decided to leave them unanswered. Instead, they responded, "You have to do what you feel is right."

*   *   *

Three weeks after he ended his relationship with Janel, things weren't as Tyler had expected. He called his parents hoping they might be able to help.

Tyler's mom answered the phone. Tyler sounded different than usual.

"Tyler, is everything okay?" she asked with concern.

"Not really."

"What's wrong?"

"Ever since I broke up with Janel, I feel like no one understands me. I sit in my dorm room for hours. I feel so alone—like no one cares about me. I don't feel like doing much of anything anymore."

This situation was like his problem with time—first too much time on his hands, and later, not enough time for himself; now, he went from feeling too close to Janel to feeling too alone.

Tyler's mother knew she couldn't solve Tyler's problem; she could only provide reassurance. "It sounds like you're going through a difficult time right now."

"I feel really alone. This isn't supposed to happen in college, is it?" He hoped that her answer would be a resounding no.

His mother asked, "Do you regret your decision to break up with Janel?"

"Yeah, I do. But I was afraid that I was losing my independence. I think I was wrong."

"Why don't you call her? Since you've had some time to think about things, maybe now you'll be better prepared to be in a relationship with Janel."

"Yeah, maybe you're right. I'm going to call her."

"Good luck. Be honest with her."

"I will."

Before they hung up, his mom caringly said, "You never know what might happen until you try. At the very least, you owe yourself—and each other—that."

Tyler mustered his courage and called Janel. After the awkward beginning to their conversation, they began to laugh and joke around with each other like they used to before they broke up. Then, Tyler tried to be honest with Janel about his feelings and desires.

"Janel, I have to be completely honest, I made a mistake in breaking up with you. I miss you. I overreacted about that whole space thing. I don't know what got into me. I want my independence, but I don't like being without you. Do you understand what I'm getting at? Would you give me a second chance?"

As Janel listened to Tyler, she thought she understood what he was trying to say. To her, he was saying, "I care about you, but sometimes your care can suffocate my desire for independence. Could you back off on your displays of affection so I can have a little time for myself?"

During their time apart, Janel had thought of Tyler often. She wrote daily in her journal about how much she missed him. Her roommates couldn't believe they broke up. They told her that they thought they were meant for each other. Unlike Tyler, Janel believed affection was more important than independence, but she decided to give their relationship another chance, given that it was clear how much they cared for one another.

After Janel and Tyler got back together, she lessened her expressions of interest, thinking that was what Tyler wanted. Rather than text-message him throughout the day, she text-messaged him once a week. Rather than call Tyler each day, she called every other day. Rather than think about whether he might want to eat dinner with her, she ate dinner with her friends. Rather than call him first to see what he was doing on Friday night, she called her girlfriends first to see what they were doing.

Initially, Tyler liked the arrangement. He felt it was perfect. He routinely told her, "I really like the way things are going right now. We have a nice balance."

Janel, however, didn't feel the same way. She felt that Tyler's desire for independence prevented her from being herself; but she accepted the arrangement because she couldn't ignore the fact that she cared about Tyler.

Two months later, Tyler's "too-much-too-little" problem kicked in again. But this time, Tyler accused Janel of not caring enough. He told her, "Janel, it just feels like you're never around. You would never know we were boyfriend and girlfriend. If it's going to be like this, we should go our separate ways."

*   *   *

Feeling alone and confused after breaking up with Janel for a second time, Tyler went to Johnny's, a popular bar of choice for Shadow U students.

He lamented, "One day I'm bored, the next I feel like I have no time for myself and the things I want to do. One day I really like someone, the next I feel like I need space. Then I think I've fixed my relationship and what happens? I accuse Janel of not caring enough!"

The bartender asked Tyler for his ID. Tyler pulled out his surefire fake ID to the bartender's satisfaction. "Give me a Jack and Coke," Tyler requested. While sipping his drink, he became more and more confused as he tried to understand how he was getting this whole college experience thing wrong, totally wrong. "What a life!" he said to himself out loud.

A gentleman two stools away looked up after Tyler's exasperated proclamation. The two made eye contact. Recognizing what he had said, Tyler added, "I'm sorry, I didn't mean to say that out loud."

The man, unmoved, kept staring at him. Then, in a calm voice, the man said, "I don't know who you are, but I know what you're going through."

"Huh?" Tyler responded, thinking to himself, "This guy must be drunk. Drunk people always understand. Who else would be at Johnny's on a Monday afternoon but drunks and lost students trying to find their way?"

"Tell me about what's going on," the man said.

"What do I have to lose? Maybe putting all my confusing thoughts into words will help me figure this out," Tyler thought.

"Here's the *Cliffs Notes* version," Tyler said. "I really think there's something wrong with me. One day I don't have enough of something, the next day I have it, and as soon as I get it, I feel like I have too much and want to get rid of it again. Or, one day I have too much of something, the next day I get rid of it, and then all of a sudden, I miss it! Crazy, I know, but that's the short and sweet of it, buddy."

There was a brief pause after Tyler explained his life situation in two clean sentences.

"My name is DB," the man said.

"My name is Tyler. Nice to meet you. I don't want to take any more of your time. I'm a hopeless case."

"I think I know your problem."

"If you do, you're a miracle worker. Go ahead. This will be interesting."

"You're binge thinking," he told Tyler.

Laughing in disbelief, Tyler said, "This is getting better by the minute. Binge drinking? That makes sense. I'm in a bar in the middle of the afternoon on a weekday—but that's not my problem. How many have you had this afternoon?"

"No, not binge drinking, Tyler, binge *thinking*."

"What's that mean?"

"Tyler, if you drink too much, your body lets you know. If you continue drinking Jack and Cokes all day, without food and without pacing yourself, your body will tell you that you have indulged."

"That's for sure. I would throw up all night. I hate throwing up."

"Me too," DB said. "Ironically, throwing up is a blessing, Tyler."

"A blessing?"

"Your body tells you when you've gone too far. 'Too much, Tyler,' it tells you. 'Stop now!' Your body purges itself of the poisons of excess. You can drink a lot of those Jack and Cokes, but there's a point when you've had too much. It's different for each of us, but we all have a breaking point. Your excesses are of your mind, not your body."

"My breaking point? Go on."

"Maybe another example will help you. When was the last time you went home, Tyler?"

"A month ago."

"Do you enjoy your mom's home cooking?"

"Yeah, that's one of the reasons I love going home so much. I hate the food on campus. It sucks!"

"Think about your drive home for a moment. Do you ever find yourself fantasizing about how much you're going to eat? Do you even go so far as to eat lightly at lunch before your big homecoming dinner so you can save up as much room as possible for the big meal?"

"All the time. I imagine my mom's fried chicken, mashed potatoes, corn, and homemade bread. She always makes a big meal the first night I get home. It's unbelievable."

"Think about when you get home after a long drive, after having dreamed about the big meal. There it is, all that food before you. You take that first bite, and eventually you ask for seconds—and thirds—if you're really hungry."

"Absolutely!"

"At some point, your body stops you, right?"

"I can eat a lot—don't get me wrong—but for some reason, I can never eat as much as I want or think I can."

"What stops you?"

He thought for a second, and then responded, "I feel like I'm going to be sick. I try to eat more, but my body won't let me. I slow down. I even unbutton the top button on my pants. There's always a point when I look at the food and feel like I'm going to be sick. It's weird, DB. After I pig out, the food that looked so good only minutes ago—the fried chicken, the mashed potatoes, the corn, and the homemade bread—suddenly makes me feel like I'm going to hurl."

"I know the feeling, Tyler. Your body, unlike your thoughts, can regulate itself. Even if your mind has unquenchable desires, your body can only take in so much. It has a breaking point. Your body clues you into knowing when you've eaten too much food. As you said yourself, your stomach feels like it's going to burst, and you feel nauseated. You become very sleepy. These are clear signs that too much is too much. Here's the kicker: these types of excess—too much of this and too little of that—that are driving you crazy now, are thoughts that don't clearly reveal themselves in your body. There's no clear breaking point."

Mesmerized, Tyler moved one stool closer to DB.

"Tyler, you're binging on what I call 'tortured by the too.' The problem you face is that many of your college excesses are in your head—not in your body. I know this isn't going to win me any points with your parents, but the easiest excesses in college to overcome are physical excesses. Don't get me wrong. They can be extremely dangerous. At least your body lets you know when you're binging on alcohol, getting too little sleep, exercising too much, and so forth."

"Yeah, you should've seen me last weekend. Let's just say the walk home was rough."

"You can easily tell when you've gone too far when abusing your body. When it comes to thinking, however, it's less clear, but just as unhealthy."

DB said, in a voice different than Tyler had heard before, "You and I, and everybody else for that matter, can conceive of too much or too little."

"You've lost me again."

"Let's see. How can I explain this? This is going to sound totally off topic, but have you ever visited a farm?"

"No."

"Have you ever seen a cow?"

"Yeah, sure. Who hasn't?"

"Good. Now listen very carefully. Cows *can* settle."

"What?" Tyler asked in complete confusion.

"Tyler, cows can't torture themselves with the 'too' like you and I can because they can't conceive of too much or too little. What's before them is what is before them—nothing less, nothing more. They don't look at the patch of pasture they're eating and say to the cow next to them, 'Hey, this pasture has too little color; let's not eat it.' Or when there's an endless field of pasture as far as they can see, they don't say to themselves or to another cow, 'This is too much pasture, I'm uncomfortable here. Let's go where we aren't so overwhelmed with choice.' In both cases, the cows eat the pasture before them; they don't torture themselves like we do with thoughts of too much or too little. Tyler, that's what we do all the time. We're too creative for our own good. Because you can conceive of too much and too little, you spend most of your time in college fearing the dreaded settle."

"I think I have a few more problems than some cow."

"What pushes you over into binge thinking is the great fear of the settle. The settle comes in many shapes and sizes, but it lurks in the shadows of almost all the choices you make."

"Do you have an example that doesn't involve a cow?" Tyler interjected.

"Let's say you get an eighty-eight percent on your biology midterm exam. This is a good grade, no doubt. But the idea of too little creeps into your mind, and instead of focusing on the eighty-eight percent, you obsess about the twelve percentage points you missed. You celebrate the eighty-eight percent for a nanosecond compared to the endless hours you dedicate to torturing yourself with why you didn't do better, going over the reasons why you didn't get at least an A minus. You focus on what didn't happen versus what did happen."

"I've done that, for sure. I believe trying to better yourself is a good thing. Isn't never being satisfied a good thing? I don't want my doctor ever to be content with having enough knowledge or experience. Same thing with pilots, architects, and scientists."

"The fear of settling does push us to do better, to get more, and to achieve things we previously only dreamed of. That's all well and good. The question is this, Tyler, and this is important; in fact, I want you to think about this before you respond."

Tyler sat waiting in anticipation, poised for the unexpected.

"During your college experience, have you ever awakened to your alarm clock and said to yourself, 'This is it! My life is enough! This is the very minute, this is the very second when there's neither too little nor too much.' Have you ever been content merely where you are—not trying to arrive somewhere else besides where you are then and there?"

Tyler paused and then answered, "Only old people do that. They're the only ones who have the time. They don't have anything more to do or accomplish."

"Unfortunately, being tormented by the 'too' doesn't go away as we get older."

"I'll have to believe you on that one."

"Tyler, it's not just you. People can't help but talk to themselves and others in the language of too little or too much."

"I guess I did go from having too much time on my hands to having too many things to do. And I went from having a girlfriend to having too much me time! My parents must think I'm never satisfied."

"Remember the cow example?"

"Not the cows again, DB."

"We all fear that if we accept where we are right now, if we enjoy what we're doing or whom we're dating right now, then others will accuse us of being complacent, of not caring about our future, of not reaching our potential, of missing out on something or someone better."

"Am I doomed to a life of always seeing the world as too much or too little?"

"Sadly, we don't have a vocabulary for talking about enoughness. It's hard to talk satisfaction talk. We're so afraid of jinxing ourselves. If we talk as if we have enough—a good life, a good relationship, and so forth—we fear something terrible will all of a sudden happen to us."

"It's bad karma, DB."

"For the cows, everything just *is*. Pasture is pasture. It's not too tall, too short, too green, or not green enough. It just is. A cow who gives eight gallons of milk one day won't be upset with herself if she produces only seven gallons the next day. She just walks into the barn and gets milked. She can't analyze her milk production."

"Sounds like cows aren't the only ones being milked."

"Cows don't analyze the world like we do. Tyler, we're stuck torturing ourselves by having thoughts about too much of this and too little of that. Very rarely do we recognize or allow ourselves to think in the mindset of enough, because if we do, we fear how others might judge us. Will they think we don't have goals? Will they think we're too confident, too sure of the value of what we've achieved? Will they think we don't want to make a better life for ourselves and our families? It's a never-ending dilemma."

"I hear you, DB, but you're not telling me how to fix the 'too' stuff."

"There is a way to help you when you're binging on thoughts of too much or too little. I bet you have a to-do list, right?"

"Yeah, of course. If I didn't, I wouldn't be able to remember all the things I have to do each week."

"Great. To-do lists and organizers focus your attention on the concept of too little—that is, what you haven't done yet. This isn't bad. But in the process of obsessing about what isn't enough or what we haven't done, we forget what has been done, what has been accomplished, what we do have. Now create another list—not a to-do list, but a *to-did* list."

"A to-did list?"

"I know it sounds funny, but stick with me. Your to-did list reminds you of what you've accomplished, that you did get an eighty-eight percent, that you do have friends you enjoy spending time with, and so forth. Your to-do list focuses your attention on the not-enough or too-little aspects of your existence. Conversely, the to-did list focuses your attention on the enough aspects of your existence. Always make sure you fill these out together, never alone. The to-do list needs to be restrained. If you only have a to-do list, you will think only in terms of not enough and too little. There's always something more to do. If you don't remember what you've accomplished, you'll end up feeling inadequate."

Tyler was lost in deep thought as he sat sipping his Jack and Coke. As Tyler was contemplating DB's idea of having both a to-do list *and* a to-did list, he turned to ask DB how he knew so much about the stress of dissatisfaction, but DB was gone. Tyler then turned to the bartender and asked where the guy he was talking to had gone.

The bartender said with a wry smile, "Oh, he always disappears without notice."

"How much for my drink?" Tyler asked.

"It's on the house, buddy. Anyone who drinks with DB gets his drinks free."

"Why?"

Before the bartender had time to answer, he was interrupted by another Shadow U student's order.

As Tyler sat alone at the bar, he thought about how much better he felt after having talked to DB. He knew his situation hadn't changed since he first walked into Johnny's, but he also knew something was different. He thought to himself, "Maybe I don't have too many burdens. Maybe DB was right and I was drunk on thoughts of too much and too little."

Moment Abuser Maya

"Dreaming of the future is the currency of choice in college."

Maya was the ideal college student. Her friends thought she was perfect. Parents loved Maya. They used her as an example of what they wanted their daughters and sons to become. Professors loved Maya. They used her as an example of academic achievement. Shadow U loved Maya. She was their model college student. She was even featured in the Shadow U brochure sent to prospective students. She was the poster child for what every college hoped students could be and what every student envied. What wasn't there to respect and admire about Maya? She had a 4.0 grade point average and made the dean's list each and every semester. But beyond grades, there was something else that distinguished Maya from other students.

Most students dreaded the first day of class when professors attempted to get to know their students by asking questions about their majors and, of course, what they wanted to do after graduation. Not Maya. She embraced the first day of class.

Embarrassed and unsure of their lives after college, most students reluctantly responded to professors' inquiries with something like, "My name is Malcolm, and I'm…undecided about my major. What am I going to do after graduation? Uh…well, I'm not sure."

Unlike her peers, Maya was resolute. She knew what she wanted to become. When professors asked her about her future, in one proud and boastful breath, she would say, "Hi, my name is Maya. I'm a political science major. After college, I will attend law school. After that, I will become a lawyer. And ultimately, I will be a senator."

Some students admired Maya because she shared her aspirations with such force and clarity. Some students despised her arrogance and unwavering assurance. Regardless of what her fellow students thought of her, all agreed that Maya's future appeared to be a done deal.

*   *   *

Maya wasn't always like this. She used to be like everyone else. During her first semester at Shadow U, she was, like her peers, indecisive about her future. She had more immediate issues to resolve. Everything was new. She was trying to balance a full load of classes with demanding professors who all acted as if their class was the most important class. On top of that, Maya was trying to adjust to living away from home. She had the hardest time adjusting to living in the dorms. She hated the meals in the cafeteria; more often than not, her showers were cold; and to top it off, she wasn't getting enough sleep because her roommate stayed up late at night talking on the phone. During her first semester, Maya was consumed with simply surviving.

That first semester, Maya couldn't wait to return home for Thanksgiving. She thought, "For four days, I can just relax, forget about the stresses of school, and enjoy the luxuries of home that I've so missed."

Within two hours of arriving home for Thanksgiving, however, things weren't as she expected. Her uncle, who was visiting for Thanksgiving, bombarded her with questions. "Maya, how's your first year of college going?" Before she could answer, he asked another question. "What's your major?"

"I think I want to be a political science major."

He repeated her words, but this time in question form. "Political science? Huh. What do you want to do with that?" The questions just kept coming.

She thought, "I'm at home. Why am I being attacked here, of all places? Home is supposed to be a refuge. I'm just trying to survive in college; who in their right mind expects me to know what I want to do after graduation? I don't even know what I'm doing next week." She finally said in a slow and deliberate voice, "I don't know what I'm going to do with political science. I haven't thought about it."

"Maya," he rebutted. "I'm curious, really. What kinds of jobs do political science majors get after graduation?"

She slowly repeated the last part of the question. "After graduation? Uh...I don't know."

"Hey, everyone," her uncle joked, "Maya's going to live off her parents forever. Maya, do you really need to pay thousands of dollars a year to end up at home again?"

Everyone laughed except Maya. The rest of her break didn't improve.

Maya's uncle thought she should be a business major. "At least you would get a real job instead of one of those liberal artsy-fartsy majors that lead nowhere," he said.

Maya's grandfather thought she should be a teacher. Unsolicited, he said to Maya, "You're so patient and kind, and you like working with kids."

Maya's mom thought she should be a nurse. "You're a great caretaker, Maya. Don't you think that would be a natural fit? It doesn't hurt that there's a national shortage of nurses."

And so on and so forth.

As she listened to her future through the voices of her relatives, Maya knew things had to change. She promised herself that her Thanksgiving disaster would never be repeated. "Never again will I be embarrassed liked this," she resolved.

*   *   *

Later that school year, Maya visited her roommate's home three hours away from Shadow U. After a wonderful home-cooked meal, the inevitable happened. Her friend's parents asked her in a sincere and caring tone, "Maya, what's your major?"

She pounced on their question without hesitation: "I'm a political science major."

"How nice," the doting parents said.

Maya wasn't finished. She simply paused for effect. She added with confidence, "In order to go to law school, so I can become a lawyer, and eventually a senator."

Silence ensued for what seemed like minutes.

Maya asked herself, "Did I say something wrong?"

Just as this thought raced through her head, she was greeted with unprecedented accolades and attention. Her friend's parents responded, "Wow, you really know where you're going in life."

Then the parents turned to their daughter and said, "Why can't you have clear goals like Maya? She knows what she wants to do."

Maya had the secret formula to college success down pat. She repeated it to herself over and over on the drive home from her friend's house. She thought, "When I talk of my future with certainty, when I talk big about what I'm going to do and who I'm going to become, people respect me. People treat me differently."

Not only did Maya become book smart early in college, she also became college smart. During her first year of college, she learned that the more certain her future seemed, the more others respected her. She knew that one of the reasons she was going to college was to better herself. She knew she wasn't alone. Whether they acknowledged it or not, she knew anyone who spent all that time and energy getting into college—anyone who dedicated themselves to all-nighters and boring lectures while in college—had to be interested in bettering their future.

She thought, "If people go to college to know more, to earn more money after graduation, and to do better in life, then getting attention and admiration means more than simply what you do in college. If I act and talk as if the present is simply a dress rehearsal for the future, students, professors, and parents will treat me as if I'm successful!" Maya's secret mantra was set in stone: dream big, talk a lot about your future, watch the respect and admiration flow. "Easy. Too easy," she thought.

For the remainder of her time in college, Maya set out to earn the respect of her peers and professors. She figured out that all she had to do was add "in order to" to everything she said. In the process, her entire college existence became consumed with talking, acting, and thinking with the phrase "in order to" in the midst of everything she said, did, and thought. What began as a means of impressing others became a way of life for Maya. Nothing she did was done without a future justification. Maya didn't stay up all night cramming for her finals to learn more. She stayed up all night cramming in order to qualify for her major. Maya didn't join numerous organizations to meet people and become active. She joined in order to prove to others that she could be a good leader. Maya didn't acquire an internship at a law office to learn about law. No, that would be pointless. She acquired an internship in order to improve her chances of being accepted by a prestigious law school. Maya became so good at "in ordering to" her everyday existence that her future became more real than her present.

*   *   *

Maya felt most comfortable at the Shadow U Career Center. Everybody at the Career Center knew Maya. She was only a sophomore, but because the future was more real to her than the present, it was one of the few places on campus where she felt she belonged.

During one fateful visit to the Career Center, Maya picked up a book she had ordered. "Hi, Maya. Nice to see you again. Only two visits to the Career Center this week? You must be having a busy week," said Linda, a career counselor.

"Yeah, ever since I took over as student president of the Future Lawyers of America, I haven't had much free time! Oh well, all this work will pay off in the end."

Linda heard this kind of talk from Maya each week. She loved giving Maya a hard time. Usually, it was Linda who helped students think about their futures, but Maya was a unique case. She practically ran the Career Center for herself. She was doing everything necessary to secure her future. Maya had already taken three different types of personality tests to determine her ideal occupation. All three tests indicated she should pursue a career in law. She had already completed a résumé workshop and had interviewed several lawyers to ensure that being a lawyer was the right profession for her. She had even interviewed a senator on a visit to Washington, D.C., just to make sure the life of a senator would fit her. She had her future all figured out before most of her peers had even started thinking about life after graduation.

Whenever Maya visited the Career Center, Linda joked with her, but Maya had little time to laugh. "Maya, when was the last time you went on a date?"

Maya responded, "Date? What are you talking about, Linda? You know I don't have time for dates. I have too many things I have to do. Besides, guys would just get in the way of my dreams. I don't want to meet someone right now. I'm not ready—I mean—they're not ready for me!"

"Maya, when was the last time you just hung out?"

"Linda, you don't get it, do you? Hang out? If I hang out with someone, they'll end up distracting me. Going on dates and hanging out with friends isn't rewarded in college."

Linda had come to expect this kind of response. Maya had no more time for small talk. She cut Linda off to ask, "Hey, did that book I had you order finally arrive?"

"Actually, it did."

"Finally!" Exasperated, Maya said, "I'm already behind. This book was supposed to arrive last week. I need to read it right away."

"Oh, you're behind in reading *Making Your Law Dreams Come True— A Guide for Third-Year Law Students?* Maya, don't you think you're getting ahead of yourself? You're only a sophomore."

"Thanks," Maya said, ignoring Linda's question. "I actually have a few minutes right now to look at the book."

Maya headed to her favorite chair in the Career Center, which was nestled next to countless pamphlets on law schools. As usual, she skimmed the pages of her book. She never leisurely read a book cover to cover, as she had mastered the art of speed reading.

Halfway through the book, however, something appeared that Maya couldn't have anticipated. Taped inside the book was a white envelope. Maya became curious. "Who would tape a letter inside this book?" she thought. She opened the envelope and inside was a letter. It read:

> *I don't know who you are, but I know what you're going through. In a short e-mail, please briefly explain the details of your particular situation. I can help you. Please e-mail me at dbfreeme@borgesandwhite.com.*
> *In care,*
> *DB*

Immediately, Maya walked up to Linda. "Linda, I thought you'd ordered a new book!"

"You know our budget, Maya. We've already ordered three career-oriented books for you in the past month. My supervisor told me to cut costs, so I ordered a used book. The person I ordered it from online had a four-star rating. Is there something wrong with the book?"

"Uhh, yeah."

"What?"

"I think somebody named DB accidentally left a personal letter in the book. There's an e-mail address in the letter. I'll send an e-mail to let this DB know about the misplaced letter." Before Maya left the Career Center, she e-mailed DB. She wrote:

> *Dear DB,*
> *I have the book you sold to the Shadow U Career Center. The title of the book is Making Your Law Dreams Come True—A Guide for Third-Year Law Students. You accidentally left a personal letter in the book. I can return it to you. Just provide your address and I will send it to you immediately.*
> *Maya*

She quickly logged out, said goodbye to Linda, and with book in hand, headed out to prepare for her future.

Later that evening, during a break from her study group, Maya checked her e-mail. She was expecting a response from a prestigious lawyer who worked at a law firm she had contacted. She hoped to acquire a summer internship in his firm's main office and wanted to know whether it would be worth her time. As she scrolled down and deleted junk mail in rapid-fire succession, looking for the lawyer's e-mail address, she came upon an e-mail address that read: dbfreeme@borgesandwhite.com. That address caught her attention. "Oh yeah," she thought. "This must be about that letter." She opened the e-mail. She thought DB was simply going to make the obligatory apology and then provide an address so she could return the personal note. Instead, she was surprised to read:

> *Dear Maya,*
> *The letter was for you. If you can fit me into your schedule, be online tonight at 8 p.m. and we can continue this conversation over IM since I bet you don't have time to meet in person.*
> *In care,*
> *DB*

"What a joke," she thought. "Why would I instant message a complete stranger? What's in this for me?"

After Maya's study session was over, she did something she hadn't done in a long time: she did something without justification. She assumed she wouldn't gain anything from her conversation with DB, but she decided to see if he would instant message her as he said he would. In a twisted way, unique to Maya, she felt as if she were living life on the edge.

Maya logged on at the assigned time, and within minutes, she received an instant message from dbfreeme. Even though Maya was living on the edge, she didn't show it. She typed furiously and bluntly, "Who do you think you are, wasting my time like this? Meeting for the sake of meeting, who has time for that?"

DB responded, "Hello, Maya, nice to meet your virtual self."

Not more than three seconds passed before Maya shot back, "I'm very busy. I have things to do. Unlike you, I don't have time to meet random people online."

"Nice to meet you too, Maya. You're the fastest typist I've ever chatted with. This shouldn't last too long. I hope I can keep up."

The rest of the conversation occurred as follows:

dbfreeme	Maya, I'm not a random person and this isn't a random meeting.
Mayaluvslaw	Not random? Are you stalking me?
dbfreeme	Not at all.
Mayaluvslaw	Who are you then?
dbfreeme	I'm the former owner of the book you got from the Career Center.
Mayaluvslaw	Why were you expecting my e-mail?
dbfreeme	Maya, what and who are you in a hurry to become?
Mayaluvslaw	What are you talking about? Do you mean what do I want to do with my life?
dbfreeme	That will do.
Mayaluvslaw	If that's your question, I want to be a lawyer in order to become a senator.
dbfreeme	I figured that because you found my letter taped inside the book. Tell me something more about yourself.
Mayaluvslaw	Hey, if you think I'm into that cyber stuff, you're crazy.
dbfreeme	No, Maya, tell me something about your college experience.
Mayaluvslaw	If you must know, I was on the dean's list last year. I got straight As. I'm at the top of my class. I just became student president of the Future Lawyers of America. I'm going to take the practice

	LSAT in a week. I'm waiting for a reply about an internship opportunity with a prestigious law firm in New York. I want to be in public service—I want to be a senator. Why do you care?
dbfreeme	I'm sorry, Maya.
Mayaluvslaw	You're sorry? What are you talking about? No one feels sorry for me. I'm well-liked at Shadow U. Professors respect me. Parents love me.
dbfreeme	Maya, that's all very impressive, but tell me something else about yourself—and this time you can't refer to the past.
Mayaluvslaw	You want me to play a game? I don't play games.
dbfreeme	Just this once, Maya. I have a feeling this game will be short.
Mayaluvslaw	Fine. Okay, nothing about the past. I'm going to graduate a semester early. I'm going to graduate first in my class. I will be the valedictorian. I will have my choice of law schools. Oh yeah, and I will drive a Beamer by the time I'm 30.
dbfreeme	One more thing. Tell me about yourself, but this time, you can't talk about the past or future.

Mayaluvslaw	What? That's not fair. If I can't talk about the past or future, there's nothing to say.
dbfreeme	This game was shorter than I thought.
Mayaluvslaw	What's the point of this game?
dbfreeme	The point? Maya, you're what I call a "moment abuser"—and perhaps one of the worst cases I've seen in years.
Mayaluvslaw	A moment abuser? You're crazy. I don't know what you're talking about.
dbfreeme	Who did you talk to today?
Mayaluvslaw	I don't remember. That's not important. I spent most of my day reading up on my future law career.
dbfreeme	I know. Remember, I once owned that book. What did you think about today?
Mayaluvslaw	What law school I was going to attend. What kind of law I want to study. I can't decide between civil-rights or environmental law. I also thought about my first-year salary.
dbfreeme	Yes, you have all the symptoms of a moment abuser. No doubt about it. Maya, the short game we just played—did you notice anything?
Mayaluvslaw	Yeah, it was pointless.

dbfreeme	I should've expected that answer. No, it wasn't pointless. When I asked you to tell me about yourself, you had plenty to say. When I told you that you couldn't talk about the past, you talked about yourself in the future.
Mayaluvslaw	So?
dbfreeme	Here's the kicker. When I asked you to tell me about yourself— and then restricted you from using the past and future tenses— you had nothing to say.
Mayaluvslaw	I don't understand what you're asking. I don't know how to talk about the present. Talking about the present makes no sense.
dbfreeme	Exactly. Maya, I'm afraid you don't have the right training.
Mayaluvslaw	What? I don't have the right training? Impossible. I'm the most well-trained and well-prepared student at Shadow U. You don't know me.
dbfreeme	I don't doubt that you're the most well-trained and well-prepared student for your future. Everything you do, everything you say, everything you think about is in preparation for the future. You're also the most unequipped and unprepared stu-

dent for your present I have ever met. Nothing you do, nothing you say, nothing you think is about now.

Mayaluvslaw   So what?

dbfreeme   You've become too focused on thinking and talking about your future that nothing else matters. One day blurs into the next because everything you do is in preparation for something else. Can you enjoy sitting in the park enjoying the sun or do you feel guilty because you should be doing something productive? Can you go for a leisurely walk without worrying about how much studying you still have to do? Can you enjoy reading a good book without underlining or taking notes?

Mayaluvslaw   That's why I'm in college. To prepare myself for life. Tell me something I don't know.

dbfreeme   In the process of preparing yourself for life, you're making yourself unprepared for living.

Mayaluvslaw   No one cares about what you're doing now in college. It's all about who you're going to become.

dbfreeme   I can tell you're still not convinced. I'm not surprised. One more question for you. Do you think you'll fulfill your dreams?

Mayaluvslaw	Yes. That's the only thing I do know. Of course, there are a lot of people around here who don't want me to succeed. My roommate is always bugging me about going out. And students in some of my classes ask the stupidest questions. Their questions are never related to the subject at hand. They annoy me to no end.
dbfreeme	Sounds like you have an uphill battle—a lot of obstacles to overcome.
Mayaluvslaw	Finally, someone understands.
dbfreeme	If your entire college existence is devoted to your future, it's no surprise you think so many people are getting in the way of who you want to become and what you want to do. Maya, you don't spend much time in the present because the present only reminds you of what you're NOT doing.
Mayaluvslaw	I don't know what you're talking about. I'm just trying to do the things I need to do in order to get to the stuff in my life that's really important.
dbfreeme	Everything in your life now is in preparation for tomorrow. I don't blame you. I've just never seen someone do it as well as you. Dreaming of the future is the

currency of choice in college. You're rich! In college, you're rewarded and admired for your moment abuse. You've become the perfect perpetual planner, Maya. Congratulations. But have you ever paused long enough to consider how much you're a product of your college environment?

Mayaluvslaw

I'm making myself a valuable product for life after college.

dbfreeme

By focusing exclusively on the future, you've left no room for your present.

Mayaluvslaw

Sounds like you're obsessed with all this new-age junk—live in the moment crap that only unsuccessful people like to talk about. Don't tell me you're one of those Zen guys. Being in the moment sounds really nice; but I've noticed the people who talk about being in the moment never have real jobs. They're always yoga instructors or something funky like that. Sounds good, but they're not lawyers or senators.

dbfreeme

Before you jump to conclusions, consider for a moment how you think and talk. Do you ever think

	or talk about the present without the future getting in the way?
Mayaluvslaw	My future doesn't get in my way.
dbfreeme	A lot of the time we can't help but speak to our future: what is going to happen—what we hope will happen—what we plan to happen. But because you have so efficiently trained yourself *out* of the moment, all you know how to talk about is what is *going* to happen and what *should* happen.
Mayaluvslaw	People who spend all their time talking about the present don't succeed in college.
dbfreeme	You have a point, but you're not entirely correct. It's important to think about your future, and it's fun to dream about what you want to do and who you want to become. College does reward students who perpetually plan for their future. But what about who you are now? Always talking about your future not only means you don't know how to talk about the present, but it also means you don't think much of yourself *without* your dreams—who you're going to be, how much money you're going to make.
dbfreeme	Maya, still there?

Mayaluvslaw	Sorry. I was just thinking. You're right, I don't talk about who I am without adding something about what or who I'm going to become. I think I do it so much because it works.
dbfreeme	I'm sure it does, but in the process, you also get stuck in the future.
Mayaluvslaw	You can't get stuck in the future. That's impossible.
dbfreeme	Because we can contemplate tomorrow, it's possible. In your case, not only is it possible, it's inevitable. You've been so focused on defining yourself by who you're going to be and what you're going to do that it becomes impossible to catch up with yourself.
Mayaluvslaw	Stop speaking in riddles.
dbfreeme	If you go to law school, become a lawyer, and then become a senator, you'll still be ahead of yourself. You still won't be satisfied. There still will be something else to do, something more to achieve. Your accomplishments will never be good enough.
Mayaluvslaw	If I become a lawyer and then a senator—I'll have made it!
dbfreeme	Really? That's interesting. So then you'll be done obsessing about the

	future? That would be quite a turnaround. You won't want to accomplish anything else after you become a senator?
Mayaluvslaw	If I make it that far, why not go all the way—the U.S. Supreme Court, or maybe the presidency?
dbfreeme	That's what I thought. If you're not careful and you continue obsessing about your future, your present will become a dream.
Mayaluvslaw	I can tell you're after something.
dbfreeme	There's something you can try.
Mayaluvslaw	What?
dbfreeme	What I'm going to ask you to try is going to be tough—and you're going to feel a bit weird trying it. In fact, it might even make you feel bad—literally sick. Before you're able to enjoy your present, you'll first have to purge yourself of your obsession with the future.
Mayaluvslaw	I have to throw up?
dbfreeme	Not literally. For a week, I want you to temporarily put on hold the activities you would normally participate in only because you want to get into law school, become a lawyer, and so forth.
Mayaluvslaw	I don't get it. What's that going to do? Won't I just be miserable? What will I do?

dbfreeme

That's my point. Without making your present bend to your future, you have to figure out what your present is good for. Maya, I'm warning you, this is going to be difficult. I'm asking you to temporarily suspend your thoughts about your future. Your job is to figure out how to live now without worrying about how your life will be better in ten years.

Mayaluvslaw

DB, you must be unemployed. What do you do anyway? How do you make a living?

dbfreeme

I don't know how to answer that question.

Mayaluvslaw

Only someone who's unemployed would encourage me to be lazy.

dbfreeme

Just because I'm taking away your reason for the present doesn't mean your present should have no purpose. Actually, it's the opposite. Once you stop looking to your future, you might be pleasantly surprised to notice what appears before you now, in the present.

Mayaluvslaw

Sounds a little weird, but I might as well try it, even though I won't have any reason to do anything. Why would I bother to get up early in the morning?

dbfreeme	I can't answer that for you, Maya. That's something you'll have to try and figure out. I do have a suggestion that might help you stay more focused on the present. In order to appreciate the present without the future always getting in the way, you need to make your thoughts obey your body rather than your body obey your thoughts of the future.
Mayaluvslaw	Huh?
dbfreeme	Like right now, you're not being aggressively present. You're probably thinking about what you need to do before you can go to sleep tonight. In fact, I bet you're thinking right now, in the middle of our conversation, about how you're going to do the exercise we talked about and still manage all of your other activities.
Mayaluvslaw	I can't help it!
dbfreeme	You have trained yourself out of being able to be in the present. Your body trails your mind. When your body trails your mind, you don't see what is happening before you. You blind yourself to what's in front of you because your mind is five or ten years into the future.

Mayaluvslaw

How do I stop my mind from taking me away from the present?

dbfreeme

You have to be conscious of when you're doing it. At this point, what's normal to you is *not* paying attention to what is around you and in front of you, *now*. You have to pinch yourself. I know it sounds silly, but it might help. Pinch yourself when your mind is running away from your present.

Mayaluvslaw

Pinch myself. Where do you get this stuff?

dbfreeme

The little sensation of pain you feel when you pinch yourself will remind you that your body is present. Maya, you're too good at forgetting about your present self. When your body is on autopilot, your mind has the freedom to vanish into the future. By pinching yourself, you'll remind yourself to attend to your body so your mind and body are in the same place, together.

Mayaluvslaw

It sounds masochistic.

dbfreeme

No more masochistic than being in two places at once.

Mayaluvslaw

If I pinch myself, will I cure myself of moment abuse?

dbfreeme	Maya, the culture of college rewards you for abusing the moment. Thinking about who you will be and what you will be doing after graduation is so rewarded in college that it's impossible to stop planning for your future. Instead of trying to avoid moment abuse, focus on being more aware of when you've forgotten about your present because you're in such a hurry to tell yourself and others about who you're going to be and what you're going to be doing after graduation. Now, go catch it.
Mayaluvslaw	Catch what?
dbfreeme	Go chase down your mind. Find out where it is. When you catch it, then, you can start being mindfully present. I have to run myself.
Mayaluvslaw	Where do you have to go?
dbfreeme	I'm late for my yoga class.

DB immediately signed off. After seemingly confirming her suspicions about DB's employment—or lack thereof—Maya logged off. Out of habit, she moved to her next task, finishing the law book—DB's law book—she had started earlier that day in the Shadow U Career Center. She had planned on finishing the book that evening, but as she began to speed read through the final two chapters, she couldn't get DB's comments out of her head. She thought to herself, "Why am I reading this book so fast? Why am I in such a hurry?" She then realized that she hadn't considered what she would do if she wasn't always preparing for her future. For the first time in a long time, she thought about what books she would read, who she might spend her time with, and what she might do for fun if she wasn't always so absorbed with her distant future.

Addicted to Aloneness Anna

"When the world appears to be full of strangers,
the only companion you can count on is your isolation."

Anna was frustrated because everyone else in college talked as if they were having the best time of their lives. Anna couldn't say the same about her life in college. She often asked herself, "What's everyone else doing that I'm not? Is there something wrong with me?"

Frustrated, Anna sat on her favorite bench in the middle of the Shadow U campus. Her mind was at ease as her self-defeating voice waned. Unfortunately, her relief was temporary. "What did you do over spring break?" a passerby asked his friend. In a voice that could be heard from fifty yards away, he responded, "We had the best time while we were in Cancun. It was so damn cool. I don't remember half of it, but my friends tell me I had a blast! You should've been there!"

The peace of that sunny afternoon turned to torture for Anna. She felt her stomach churn. "Ugggh," she gasped to herself. "Another example of why I'm different. Great." She asked herself, "What's wrong with me? Why can't I experience this whole 'we did this and we did that' thing? This is college. That 'we' thing is supposed to happen to everyone! I want to be a part of something; but here I am, just me, myself, and I!"

When Anna's peers asked her about her spring breaks, she inevitably stumbled and stuttered, replying, "Oh, you know, I just caught up on some sleep, worked a bit, read a little, and spent time with my family." Her classmates returned blank stares and "I'm sorry" looks. This fueled

Anna's self-questioning: "I never use the right words around them, or the words I use never have the right audience." She was ashamed of her spring break experiences. She had no best times to report, making her feel as if she had nothing exciting to share with others.

Anna interrogated herself to no end: "Why isn't college the best time of my life like it seems to be for so many of the people around me? Are my friends always lying? Do I not know how to make up a good story? Maybe I'm just really boring? I hope that's not it!"

While sitting, she saw Juan walk by. When she was a sophomore, she had dated Juan for three months. She smiled just thinking about their conversations. She always laughed with him. They had never really broken up; it had just kind of fizzled out. No hard feelings. But Juan did find someone else. Anna heard from a classmate that Juan was dating a girl he'd met in sociology class.

"Why would Juan want to talk to me now?" she pondered. "He's in a relationship and I'm not. We have nothing in common anymore. Ahh…to be in a relationship. That would be great! That would give me something to talk about with others, especially my roommates. They're always talking about their relationships. I would finally be able to participate in the *first* this and *first* that conversations that they make such a big deal out of—the first kiss, the first hand-holding experience, and the first time someone you care about says, 'I love you.'"

Thinking this way didn't help. Anna's body slumped as she watched fellow students walk by. The more people she saw, the more alone she felt. The more alone she felt, the more her body slumped. Her frustration turned to sadness. As she watched her fellow students interact, she wondered if anyone even noticed her. She couldn't restrain the nasty, tyrannizing thoughts she subjected herself to until she was rescued by a voice other than her own.

"Hey, Anna, how are you? It's been too long. What have you been up to?"

"What's going on, Celina. Has it really been two years since we had chemistry class together? Time goes by so fast."

"I've got to go, I'm late for class," Celina said. She added, "But we should get together. My neighbor is having a party this Thursday. It'll be fun. We're juniors, we've earned the right to have some time off from studying." Without enough time to consider the countless reasons why she shouldn't go with Celina, Anna agreed, hoping that she might be able to get out of her funk. She promised herself she would have a good time.

*   *   *

Minutes before they went to the party, while waiting in her apartment for Celina to arrive, Anna stood in front of her mirror, not to realign her skirt and shape her hair, but to remind herself to have a good time. Anna was unsure about what a good time meant, but she knew that if she could avoid asking herself why she was so different than everyone else, she would have more than a good time; she would have a great time.

The party was overflowing. Wearing smiles, Anna and Celina walked around the apartment and engaged in social reconnaissance.

"Anna, look at him, he's cute. He's laughing with his friends. That's a plus. I know the people he's talking to. Let's go." Celina walked over to introduce Anna and herself. A big knot filled Anna's throat. Her hands began to perspire and shake. She lunged forward to grab Celina's arm, stopping her cold in her tracks. "No, I can't talk to him. I don't know him. That will be too awkward. Anyway, he's too young. He looks like he's a freshman."

"Okay, okay. Relax," replied Celina. "There are plenty more opportunities." Anna and Celina chatted about nothing serious. As they talked, they surveyed the crowd.

Anna's self-doubting internal voice reemerged: "Celina is fearless. Wherever she looks she sees a reason to introduce herself. How can she be so confident?"

"What about them?" Celina said pointing to a group toward the back of the apartment.

"No way. I don't want to talk to them. They're too alternative for me. I don't talk to people who have more than two tattoos," answered Anna with a smirk, believing that such a gesture would deflate some of the tension building between them. Anna was right about the tension. Celina wanted to meet people, and with every reason Anna constructed not to participate, she regretted inviting Anna. Celina thought, "I would've come by myself if I had known I had invited Miss No."

Anna's preference for spectating frustrated Celina. Celina maintained her composure by continuing to look around the apartment. She thought, "We have so much in common. We're all stressed out because of school. Everyone at this party wants to have a good time. How can Anna not want to be a part of all this?" Celina pointed to a group sitting in the corner as if to say "Let's go over there," thinking that perhaps Anna would be more comfortable sitting down while talking.

Anna initially agreed. She walked over with Celina. Before they introduced themselves, Anna grabbed Celina's arm again and said, "No. We can't make fools out of ourselves. They're clearly out of our league. What will they think if we approach them?"

Celina pulled her arm back and turned to Anna. "I invited you because I thought we would have fun meeting people like us. We're all Shadow U students. There are tons of cute guys here, too. What more do you want? I'm not going to sit around and come up with reasons why we shouldn't speak to people. I'll leave that to you."

Celina advanced to introduce herself. Anna stood in the middle of the crowd. She had never felt more alone than she did at that moment. Anna was her old self again. Her experience at the party matched her park bench experience and her familiar doubts returned: "I'm in the same funk that I promised myself I would get out of. I'm helpless." She realized that the only time she fit in was when she was by herself. The presence of others caused her to retreat into herself. The more people who surrounded her, the more Anna felt alone.

She left the party without saying goodbye to Celina. On her walk home, Anna abused herself with questions of why and what. "Why me? Why is this happening to me? What am I doing wrong? Why do I feel so alone when everyone else seems to fit in? What are these people doing that I'm not?" She would have cried but for the fact that she was so angry. She decided to feed her pain at Donna's, a diner near campus.

Sitting alone and distraught in a booth, she ordered a greasy burger, fries, and milk shake. She sat in silence staring at nothing but her food. When the waitress came over to ask her how the food was, Anna mumbled, "Fine, but it doesn't matter."

"Are you sure you're okay?" the waitress asked.

"Okay? No…but I am sure there's something wrong with me though. I don't know how to talk to anyone, even people I want to talk to."

The waitress countered, "That's odd. You're talking to me just fine."

"No, you don't get it. I can't explain it even if I wanted to."

After Anna had finished her meal, the waitress approached her table and said, "Honey, that nice gentleman over there said your meal was on him. The only thing he wants in return is for you to read what's written on this napkin." Before Anna could protest, the waitress walked to another table. Anna was afraid to look up. "Who paid for my meal?" she wondered, keeping her eyes focused on the napkin. "And why?" The crumpled napkin read:

> *I don't know you, but I know what you're going through. Come talk to me. I'm two booths to your left. I can help you.*
> *In care,*
> *DB*

"Oh great!" Anna thought. "What is already a horrendous night is getting worse. Now it's going to be topped off with some wacko pervert making a move on me. This is all I need!"

Anna got the attention of the waitress: "How much was my bill? I don't want that guy to pay for it. He's weird." She showed the waitress what he had written as proof.

In a southern accent that exuded both care and exasperation, the waitress responded, "Honey, of all the people in the world, you shouldn't be afraid of DB. He's been coming to Donna's for years. He talks and jokes with a lot of Shadow U students who hang out here."

"That's nice, but he's still a stranger and I don't accept money from strangers. Could you please return his money and give me my bill?"

"Stranger?" the waitress laughed. "Stranger?" she repeated mockingly. "Honey, who do you think I am? Do you know me? Why is he a stranger and not me? DB's a saint. He ain't going to hurt you, Honey. Oh, by the way, good ol' DB asks one more thing of you."

"Are you kidding me? What kind of sick conspiracy am I a part of tonight? What does this strange man want?" she thought. The waitress dropped another napkin in front of her. Anna unfolded it. It read:

> *Do you want to be more like the little boy in the next booth?*
> *If so, walk two booths over and let's talk.*
> *In care,*
> *DB*

For the first time since sitting down, Anna scanned the diner. From her point of view, she saw slackers, drunks, smart kids, and a bunch of people you would expect to see in a diner at 1 a.m. Then she saw the little boy the strange man was referring to. Her first thought was, "What kind of parents would allow a child to be in a diner at 1 a.m.?" After her initial shock, she watched the little boy as he wandered away from his parents' booth. He was no more than two years old. His walk was hesitant and wobbly, for sure. But he was adventurous. Unfazed by those he approached, he walked up to each booth with a smile on his face. At each booth, he waved and said "Hi." Each time, his "Hi" was returned with laughter and smiles. It didn't matter who it was—he always received the same result: smiles.

"Why would this strange guy want me to watch this kid?" And then, with a sinking feeling, Anna thought of her experiences only minutes earlier at the party. She realized, "I didn't approach anybody. I just tortured myself. Why? How can this little boy have no fear when he approaches strange people, while I don't even say 'hello' to other Shadow U students?"

As she was trying to figure out how the little boy was able to do what she couldn't, she acquiesced. "Maybe this guy DB can help," she thought. "What do I have to lose in talking to a guy who writes on napkins and seems to have won over my waitress? I'm in a public place. What harm can there be?" She hesitantly walked two booths over, hoping to receive a sign of reassurance from someone telling her she was doing the right thing.

Before she could change her mind, DB said, "Nobody is going to tell you to sit down; you must come to that conclusion yourself."

Startled by DB's assessment of her thoughts, she asked, "Who are you?"

"My name is DB. And your name is…?"

"Anna. Why do you want to talk to me?"

Cutting her off, DB said with a laugh, "Isn't it obvious?"

"Why did you have the waitress send over those napkins?"

"For one thing, I knew it was the only way to get your attention."

"Why do you want my attention? I don't know who you are. You're a stranger, I've never seen you before."

"That's true, you've never seen me before, but am I really a stranger?"

"Yeah, you are. You're strange. You wrote on a napkin telling me you understand me. That's beyond strange."

"Good point. I must confess that I have a bad habit of listening to other people's conversations. I couldn't help myself from overhearing what you said to the waitress."

"You overheard me say that there was something wrong with me?"

"Yes, and something else. Anna, what came to your mind when you watched the little boy?"

Still suspicious of DB's intentions, Anna cautiously answered as she sat down in DB's booth, "At first, I couldn't believe he was approaching people as if he knew them, even though I know he doesn't know anyone in this diner."

"What do you mean he doesn't know anyone?"

"They're all strangers! I mean, there's no way any of these people know each other…can't you see everybody in this diner is different? Those over in the right-hand corner of the diner, those are the cool people. Just look at what they're wearing, everything about them reeks of coolness. That group near the aisle, those are the smart kids. Every one of them has a 4.0. And the people by the door, they're slackers. They hang around this place day and night and do nothing but drink coffee, smoke, and once in awhile, they'll go outside to play hackey sack."

"Very impressive assessment, Anna. And to which group do you belong?"

After a slight pause, Anna replied, "Me? I don't belong to any of them." She eventually mustered up the courage to admit, "Sometimes it feels as if the only thing I belong to is myself."

"Congratulations, Anna, you've successfully divided everybody in this diner into clear and distinct categories. Bravo!"

Anna didn't know whether DB was commending or mocking her. She kept a confused look on her face.

"Anna, is there any chance these people you divided into groups might have something in common? In other words, can you see sameness among the cool people, smart kids, and slackers?"

Anna sat in silence. She could only see them through the lens of her distinct categories. She was stuck, unable to look at them as being anything but different from each other—and especially her.

DB searched his pockets and found one blue pen and one red pen. On a napkin, he drew a red circle, a red triangle, a blue circle, and a blue triangle. He slid the napkin to Anna. She looked at it without great interest.

"Please, not another napkin."

"Anna, do me a favor and group these."

"Wait a second, this is a trick question. They can be organized by shape or color. It depends on what standard you use."

"Really?" DB replied with a grin.

"Yeah, if you use color as the standard, then you put the red circle and red triangle in one category and the blue circle and blue triangle in the other. If you use shape as the standard, then both circles go in one category and both triangles in another. It depends."

"Anna, please correct me if I'm wrong, but I hear you saying that whether something is different or the same depends on which standard you use?"

"At least when it comes to shapes and colors," Anna said reluctantly.

"Couldn't the same type of thinking be applied to how you see and categorize people? The people in this diner who appear so different— can't they also be similar?"

Anna still wasn't convinced of DB's assertion.

"The major distinction between you and that young boy is this, Anna: when it comes to seeing people, you strictly see difference and he only sees sameness. Because you exclusively recognize difference, you can't see commonality. Commonality isn't hiding. It stares you in the face but is invisible when you only pay attention to difference. You're so locked into seeing the world from the perspective of difference that you blind yourself to anything else."

"But I do see difference, DB. Are you saying I'm making things up when I see the cool people, smart kids, and slackers as being different?"

"You do see difference and you are making things up. The people in this diner are different. At the same time, what you think you are seeing is a mirage. You *only* see difference; so I'm not surprised the world appears so full of contrasts to you. You have forgotten the presence of harmony. If you look at people in this diner only in terms of how they are different from you, you're lying to yourself because you refuse to recognize how these people are also alike. Let me guess, Anna, you feel alone, right?"

"Feel alone? I am alone."

"I'm not surprised, Anna. The sharper the differences you see in others, the more you'll be unable to appreciate sameness. If you just see difference and never see yourself as belonging to anything beyond yourself, there's no doubt you feel increasingly alone. That little boy can't do what you do since his capacity to categorize is so unrefined. His time will come soon enough because arranging the world into neat categories is the way we come to learn and talk about the world. This helps us organize the world around us. For the most part, good stuff! Nobody gets hurt! In extreme cases, such as yours, that blessing turns into a curse."

"You're right. I'm cursed. Sometimes I feel so alone even though I'm surrounded by so many people my age."

"Seeing difference turns into a curse when you forget how to relate. You're stuck, Anna, because you see others through a lens that recognizes only difference. When you only focus on what separates you from others, it makes sense that you feel like you're lost and unable to relate and connect with others around you. You forget that seeing difference is a habit. Your habit has become your reality. You create all kinds of reasons why you can't or shouldn't be with others."

"I guess I do come up with reasons why I shouldn't be with others, but why would I do that to myself?"

"You're a victim."

"A victim of what?"

"You're a victim of your own classifications. You've heard lectures about the dangers of discrimination, right?"

"Yeah."

"Everyone talks about the harms of being discriminated against. Have you ever thought about what categorizing does to the categorizer?"

"Where are you going with this, DB?"

"You victimize yourself when you see others only through the lens of difference. You're so good at creating difference that the only possible result is that everyone appears to be a stranger, including yourself."

"Sounds like the party I went to tonight."

"Party?"

"Before I got your napkins, I was at a party, but I wasn't having fun."

"Why not?"

"I felt like everyone else was different. I didn't think we had anything in common. I was afraid to talk to anyone."

"Anna, when you assign people to distinct categories, you separate them from you."

"Distinct categories? All I know is that I felt like I couldn't approach people even though I wanted to."

"Differences can be real, but you can never forget they are also changeable. If you want to see difference, you can find it. If you want to see sameness, you can find it, too."

"I still think there's something wrong with me."

"There's nothing wrong with you, Anna. You are, however, suffering from what I call an 'addiction to aloneness.'"

"Why would someone in their right mind be addicted to aloneness?"

"Sometimes we get stuck. If you only pay attention to difference, it's no surprise that you feel alone even when there are so many people around you. What's surprising is that you've become so comfortable with seeing the world only in terms of difference that aloneness feels natural."

"Come on, DB! You're saying I like punishing myself?"

"You don't like punishing yourself, Anna. Before tonight, you didn't even know you were punishing yourself. But when the world appears to be full of strangers, the only companion you can count on is your isolation."

"Is there anything I can do?"

"There is, Anna. Starting tomorrow, I want you to start seeing others through a lens that sees only sameness. It will be awkward and definitely uncomfortable at first. It might even be scary because you will be seeing things you never thought existed. Start small. When the urge to detect difference creeps into your head, tell yourself, 'He has a heart, I have a heart. He has two eyes, I have two eyes. He's in college, I'm in college.'"

"It can't be that simple. That seems childish."

"Sometimes being childlike isn't bad. Don't forget the little boy in the booth. It has become your habit to create barriers between yourself and others. In the process, you have become a victim of your own creativity. You have an endless array of reasons why you aren't like others. Trust me, you're very creative in separating the world. I witnessed it firsthand in this diner as you rattled off how everybody was different in a matter of seconds. Now spend that same energy seeking sameness."

He let her digest what he'd just explained. A few minutes passed before either said anything. Unceremoniously, DB broke the silence: "In class this week, leave your old lens that sees only difference back at your apartment. Walk into class and refrain from putting people into categories. Be the little boy whose lens is so unrefined that people aren't separated and categorized. Allow the particular situation to dictate your observations and insights rather than the labels you created yesterday that are probably outdated and misleading. If you do, I guarantee the world will look different."

She smiled as she imagined the possibilities of being like that happy, unburdened little boy for just a day.

He continued, "Anna, I've enjoyed our conversation and I'd like to hear about how your exercise goes. Can we meet again to discuss the outcome?"

"I don't want to disappoint you. I wouldn't get your hopes up, DB. I've been this way for a while."

"Let me be the judge of my own hopes, Anna. Let's meet here next Friday at seven o'clock."

*   *   *

Anna took DB's suggestion seriously. In class the following week, she initiated conversations with students she had previously seen as different. All week, she consciously chose to look for sameness among herself and others. She was surprised by how much she had in common with people she had previously thought were different from her. For the first time in college, she truly engaged her fellow classmates. She even started a conversation with a classmate whom she had previously thought was just an athlete, but when appreciated through the lens of sameness, she realized he was an aspiring writer like herself. Anna took off her spectator cap and participated in the game of life. Suddenly, everybody around her stopped looking like strangers. She was excited to share her newfound experience with DB. She knew he would be proud of her.

On Friday, Anna only had her English class, and then she was free for the rest of the day before her meeting with DB. Anna liked her English class. She dutifully kept up with all assigned readings, and she even read books on the additional-reading list her professor had provided. She also enjoyed writing. She completed every writing assignment in class and also wrote outside of class. Every day, Anna wrote in her personal journal; and she had written several short stories her family had encouraged her to publish. She refused, justifying her decision by telling herself, "What do they know? They aren't writers, and they're just being nice because they're family."

Most of all, Anna desired approval from her English professor. She was sure of one thing: "I need him to say, 'Go publish, Anna. You're work should be read. People would benefit tremendously from your insights.'"

She hadn't yet received that approval, yet she hoped each class might be the day—the day she would be recognized for her talent. She knew that the likelihood of her professor explicitly saying, "Go publish, Anna," was just a dream. Anna was a realist, too. She would settle for less. On every returned assignment, she looked for any signs of confirmation her professor might bestow upon her.

Anna had received a series of Bs on her essays up to that point in the semester. She interpreted these grades as saying, in effect, "You aren't a writer. Writers get As in English, not Bs." Worse yet, her Bs stood alone. There was nothing else—just a grade—not even a sliver of commentary. Not even a simple comment such as "I like your progress, Anna, keep up the good work," or "I like your introduction, work on rounding out your arguments. You're on the right track." She concluded that the lack of comments from her professor was a confirmation of her inabilities. She thought to herself: "Just tell me I stink, why don't you? At least I'll know for sure that I'll never be a writer. Don't put a freakin' B on my paper and expect me to know what kind of talent I have as a writer." She convinced herself that since there were no glorious adjectives before her grade, she was lacking in talent.

She believed that she kept receiving Bs on her writing assignments because her English professor didn't like her. Truth be told, the professor barely knew Anna's name and certainly knew nothing about her dream to be a writer. Anna overlooked this possibility. She instead thought, "How can he not know I want to be a writer?" Anna knew one thing for sure: her English professor was the ultimate judge of her writing.

That Friday morning, she received another B on her essay. Just the letter B. No other marks on the page. No adjectives. She was doubly disappointed because on the particular assignment she received back, she had committed extra hours to researching her topic and writing the paper. She believed that giving it more effort would push her over that B hump and into the A region.

After class, her internal voice became louder: "I'm a failure. I'll never be a writer." At first, she repeated these statements to herself; then she said them out loud, hoping somebody would hear. Nobody listened, except her, of course.

She stayed in her bed all afternoon, wondering why her professor wouldn't validate her as a writer. She wanted to cancel her evening meeting with DB, but realized she couldn't, since she didn't have his phone number. When Friday night arrived, she told herself she would meet him at the diner only to let him know that tonight wasn't a good night to meet. She preferred to return to her apartment to mourn in private. Ready to retreat as quickly as possible back into aloneness, she walked to the diner to tell DB their meeting was off.

*   *   *

When she arrived, she saw DB first and walked over to tell him she didn't intend to stay. As she approached the booth, he knew something was wrong.

"Hello, Anna, nice to see you. How are you doing this evening?"

"Not well. Let's postpone our meeting, okay?"

"Hold on, Anna. I've ordered some food. Please keep me company while I eat. What's wrong?"

"I'm not in the mood to talk. I just want to be alone."

"Are you upset because of the exercise I suggested last week?"

"No, not at all. That exercise actually worked. I realized how much I have in common with people around me. I stopped watching people. I stopped wondering how people might respond—I acted instead. I never knew that one of the reasons I felt so lonely was because of the way I looked at things. Only when I purposely looked for sameness did I realize how comfortable I had become with my own isolation."

"So, do you now understand that there's nothing wrong with you, Anna? You just became addicted to a way of seeing others that made it difficult for you to relate with other people."

"I do feel like I'm not so alone anymore."

"I don't understand, Anna. If the exercise worked, what's the problem?"

"It's my English class. My English professor refuses to recognize me as a writer. I want to be a writer so much; but the grades he gives me on my essays suggest I should be anything but a writer. When I get my grades back, all I can think is: 'Give it up, Anna, you aren't going to be a writer. Move on to something else.'"

DB's eyes lit up. Anna had her head down, unable to see DB's eyes.

"I should go now. I appreciate what you've done for me. I need to go."

"Wait a second," exhorted DB. "Do you notice the connection between what we discussed last week and what you just described?"

He waited for a response.

Unsure of the connection, she bluntly said, "No."

"Let me see if I can help explain how all this business of classifying based only on difference is also related to what you experienced in English class today."

Anna perked up.

"Do you recall your behavior last week when you first met me?"

"All I remember is that I felt like a failure."

"Before you sat down with me, you looked over your shoulder about three times, waiting for someone to tell you that you were doing the right thing. I then told you that no one was going to tell you to sit down. Something similar is happening in your English class."

"I don't see the connection at all."

"You previously classified your way into aloneness by seeing people as different from yourself. Then you spent a week appreciating sameness, seeing others for what they shared in common with you. Now you refuse to use that creative energy to further free yourself."

"Free myself from what?"

"You let yourself believe that your English professor operates a Geiger counter that somehow detects special people. You interpret his comments—or in this case, lack of comments—as the truth. Since he has yet to detect your special talents as a writer, you imprison yourself in self-doubt."

"I'm confident of one thing: I should forget about being a writer."

"Why are you so confident about that?"

"I'm a B writer!"

"Part of your frustration is that you intuitively know that you're a talented writer, yet you lack faith in that intuition."

"I'm not sure about anything anymore."

"Anna, a fight is going on inside of you. It's a fight between two wolves. One is faithful. Faithful trusts herself. She fosters her intuition even when it isn't recognized or validated by her English professor. The other is faithless. Faithless doesn't trust herself. She abandons her intuition because it is hers alone. This same fight is going on within all of us, even though we rarely think or talk about it."

"I don't feel like there's much of a fight going on in my head. There's an obvious winner."

"If we get public recognition, then we too often mistake others' faith in us as the truth. Like you, when we don't get the recognition we want or think we deserve, we usually abandon what we're passionate about because we can't imagine someone else's opinion being wrong or misguided."

"I think it would be a lot better if someone else 'feeds my wolf'—like my English professor."

"Anna, does your English professor know that you want to be a writer?"

"I don't know. I never thought about it, DB. Are you saying that I don't trust my intuition and desires because I'm waiting for my professor to confirm my own feelings?"

"I think you're starting to understand, Anna."

Before DB could finish, Anna continued, "I guess I'm letting my faithless wolf win because I'm reading too much into what my professor isn't saying."

"Yes, Anna. We often distrust our ideas simply because they are ours."

"That's how I feel with this whole writing thing."

"Unfortunately, we often wait for our ideas to be publicly pronounced by somebody else, knowing full well that we privately had the same thoughts but held our tongue because we lacked faith in our ideas."

"Sounds depressing."

"In a lot of ways it is. Especially when you know that your professor hasn't thought nearly as much about your grades as you have. He isn't trying to hurt you. At the same time, he probably isn't ever going to publicly acknowledge your abilities or desires. He doesn't think that much about it, Anna."

Once again, Anna felt as if he was speaking right to the heart of her experience, but she still wondered about the connection between this insight and last week's revelations.

"In light of what I shared with you last week, what I'm about to say may sound odd."

"DB, you've spent the last few minutes talking about wolves. Nothing will surprise me."

"Remember the exercise with the red circle, red triangle, blue circle, and blue triangle? You realized they could be grouped differently depending on what standard you used."

"Yeah, I remember."

"A similar lesson can apply to your current situation. The standard you currently use to assess whether you are a legitimate or illegitimate writer is that of professor confirmation and, more specifically, grades. Since you didn't receive the validation of either, you see yourself as an illegitimate writer."

"Basically."

"Anna, do you know where I'm going with this?"

"Are you asking me to reject the grades I don't like?"

"I'm not saying that grades aren't the standard colleges use. Teacher confirmation and grades fit some souls; but you must be creative in detecting standards that legitimize your aspirations. Don't mistake grades for specialness. Grades don't always equal specialness."

"Still easier said than done, DB."

"You're right. What I'm going to say may sound a bit harsh, but I'm going to say it anyway. If you wait for someone in college, like your professor, to tell you that you're special or talented, you're going to wait a long time. Sadly, telling students that they're brilliant isn't a priority of professors. Without getting into all the reasons why that may be the case, you have to learn not to mistake the current standard of evaluation for the only standard."

"What else is there?"

"There are many times when we want to do something yet wait for others to tap us on the shoulder to give us the okay, giving us the courage to know that what we're doing is the right thing to do or believe. If you wait for your professor to tell you that you're a writer, to tell you that you're talented, you might spend a lot of your time in college waiting."

"I still don't get what you're saying. Should I reject the grades that I don't like and accept the grades I do like? That sounds easy enough."

"No, it's more complex than that. The standards of evaluation you're taught in college, particularly grades, are a suitable starting point, but that's where it ends. Eventually, you need to develop and recognize additional standards that fit your unique self. You don't reject standards simply because you don't like them. You reject a particular standard because you feel, after careful consideration, that other standards deserve merit as well. The key is finding additional ways to categorize your world."

"DB, please, no more circles and triangles."

"We're back to creativity again, Anna. This is the connection I was talking about earlier between what happened in English class with your professor and what we talked about last week."

"Creativity? Connections? Where do you come up with this stuff?"

"The moment you start believing that only *one* criterion of measurement, one standard, is comprehensive and sufficient, then you start running into difficulties. Grades are an important standard, no doubt. They're recognized by your professors, university, future employers, family, and so forth. But you have to ask yourself if the grades you're receiving in English from your professor are sufficient unto themselves to determine whether you're a good writer and perhaps even more important, whether you should be a writer."

"I don't want to do something I'm not good at. I don't want to waste my time—I'm just paying attention to what my professor is telling me."

"Anna, is that really what is going on, or is that only part of it? If you seriously believe you're a writer, you'll have to look for additional feedback beyond institutional confirmation. Professor confirmation and grades are important, but are these the only standards you can use to evaluate your writing abilities and desires?"

"They're the only ones that count."

"Come on, Anna, you can do better than that."

"I'm still confused, DB. You said there was a connection between what we talked about last week and what's going on in my English class."

"In both situations, you became addicted to only one way of making sense of things. If you see others only through the lens of difference, you will feel alone. If you see others only through the lens of sameness, you won't be able to recognize how you're unique. If you wait for your English professor to tell you that your writing is brilliant, you might overlook other measures of assessing your writing abilities—like your passion and your diligence. If you only listen to yourself and disregard what other people, like your professor say, then you only pay attention to what makes you feel good and don't learn much from those who might know more than you do."

"Now that you mention it, my family loves my writing. I've always dismissed their evaluations because, you know, they're family. They have to like my stuff."

"Sounds like you've dismissed your family's evaluations without any thought and have accepted your professor's evaluations without enough thought."

"Give me a bottom line here, DB. This is a lot to take in all at once."

"I know it is, Anna. It comes down to this: there's always more than one way of seeing things. In your case, the key is knowing when to be a part of others and when to set yourself apart from others and, just as important, knowing when to listen to others and when to listen to yourself. Once you accept that there are always multiple standards of evaluation, that no one standard is *the* standard, you can begin to recognize that you have a choice in how you interpret others' evaluations. You'll have to discover for yourself, through observation and trial and error, which standards best fit the situation and your unique self."

"Is there a book that provides easy answers on when and how to do this?" Anna said with a laugh.

"Anna, you don't need a book."

"Perhaps you should write one of those self-help books, DB? It seems like you've thought a lot about this stuff."

"I don't think people would like my self-help books."

"Why not?"

"The most important challenges in life don't have clear answers that can be bullet-pointed or easily summarized."

"I'd read it even if there were no bolded terms!" Anna said half-jokingly.

"Thanks, Anna. But when you realize that there are no simple answers to this situation, just good judgments on when to be a part of others and when to set yourself apart from others, and when to listen to others and when to listen to yourself, you'll discover that your judgments are far superior to what any book can tell you."

DB then abruptly stopped talking and said to Anna, "It's late. I have to get up early in the morning. You're probably tired of hearing my voice anyway."

As DB went to the register to pay the bill, Anna reminded herself that how she sees others and who she listens to determines who she hangs out with and how she feels about herself. As Anna walked out of the diner, she passed the waitress who initially encouraged her to meet DB. Anna said to her with a grin, "Thanks, stranger."

Belongaholic Beck

"You have never said 'no' to anybody,
besides yourself, of course."

Beck had it made. Or so he thought. Three years had passed since he had first walked onto a college campus. In reality, Beck had it made long before his college days. When Beck was in sixth grade, his parents sat him down and said with the utmost sincerity, "We want the best for you. We want you to succeed. We want you to have choices in your life. If you want to get into the college of your choice, you need to get involved in clubs and organizations and begin volunteering, now. You need to let people know you like doing things for others. That's the way you get ahead in life, Beck." Beck responded with a simple and unassuming, "Okay."

In the ensuing days, months, and years, Beck closely followed his parents' advice. In seventh grade, he became captain of the math team. In eighth grade, he was the president of the student council. He did all this while earning countless badges as a Boy Scout.

Only when Beck was in high school did he realize why his parents had sat him down all those years before to impart the importance of participation and leadership. Beck's sister was seven years older. When she graduated from college, Beck was just a sophomore in high school. His sister's graduation forever changed Beck's life. On her graduation day at Shadow U, Beck noticed that only certain graduating seniors received attention. They were showered with awards and accolades. They wore special robes with special cords. They had medals hanging from their necks. When their names were announced as they walked across the stage, he heard strange words he couldn't decipher, such as "summa cum laude." When these Latin phrases were uttered, Beck couldn't help but notice that the crowd responded with "ooohs" and "ahhhs."

He noticed that the special graduating seniors who received all the attention had one thing in common: they participated in a laundry list of activities and belonged to multiple clubs and organizations. The two valedictorians who spoke at graduation were the two students who participated in the most prestigious activities and belonged to the most clubs and organizations. And the two valedictorians didn't just participate and belong—they led. They initiated the activities they participated in and directed the clubs and organizations to which they belonged.

The Shadow U president confirmed Beck's observations when he introduced the valedictorians. He said, "The two valedictorians representing this class are leaders among leaders, people who truly understand that intellectual excellence, service, and participation are the essential ingredients to success and achievement."

"Keys to success and achievement," reflected Beck. Those words spun around in his head as the two valedictorians spoke of their achievements, thanked their parents, and left everyone in the audience awestruck by everything they had accomplished.

From that day on, Beck's mission became clear. He knew that—if he wanted to be recognized and appreciated, if he wanted to stand out—he would have to prove that he could work with others, that he liked working with others, and most important, that he could lead others.

With all of the impressive activities and organizations Beck founded, belonged to, and led in high school, he was accepted into the college of his choice: Shadow U. Getting into college wasn't enough for Beck. His need to belong and lead didn't slow down with his acceptance into Shadow U.

Beck's extracurricular involvement in college was even more impressive than he could have imagined. He didn't know how easy it would be to participate, belong, and lead in college. Everywhere he turned, some club or organization encouraged him to join, and soon after, to lead. Everyone told him he was a born leader. Three years of dedication to participating and belonging paid off for Beck. He did stand apart from his peers. He participated and led more than anyone else he knew, and he was reminded of this every day.

His peers would admiringly say, "Beck, how do you do it? You never stop. Don't you ever slow down? Is there anything you don't do?" Beck brushed off their questions.

Impressed professors talked among themselves and agreed that Beck was a student who took advantage of the college experience. Some professors volunteered to write him recommendation letters for internships, jobs, and graduate school. Whatever he desired, he had the professors' backing.

Beck's parents constantly told him, "You make us so proud. We tell everyone we know how much you're doing and accomplishing at school."

Even the Shadow U president acknowledged Beck's unprecedented contributions. Why wouldn't he? Beck appeared at almost every college function, chaired the college governing council, was president of multiple organizations, volunteered as a tutor for the underprivileged, actively participated in his fraternity, inaugurated a program that paired college students with senior citizens, was in the elite honors program, and led his church's youth group.

Beck stood out because he said "yes" to everything and everyone. The only thing that distinguished one day from the next was what he said "yes" to. Why would he say "no" when saying "yes" to everything and everyone reminded him of how important he was?

"Beck, we're starting this new program to…can you help us out?"

"Sure. Let's see, I have class and meetings all day, but I can meet you at 7:30 before my meeting with…."

"Thanks, Beck, you're the best."

"Beck, we'd be honored if you'd speak to the freshman class about the importance of leadership. Can you do it?"

"Of course, the honor would be mine. How long do you want me to talk?"

"Beck, the interfraternity council wants you to run for president. We know you're already doing a lot, but it's for the good of the Greeks. What do you think?"

"Absolutely. In fact, I have some ideas that I think will change the image of fraternities and sororities. I can't wait to run."

Beck's friends joked that his voice mail should proclaim, "Hi, this is Beck. Yes, I can help you. Just leave the time and day of your club or organization meeting, and I'll be there. Thanks." Beck brushed off the jokes. "They're just jealous," he convinced himself.

On Friday nights, Beck usually had free time. Not by choice, though. He couldn't find peers to meet with him on Friday nights. His peers preferred to relax and spend time together. Unlike his peers who looked forward to Friday nights, Beck dreaded them. His phone rang off the hook throughout the week; but on Friday nights, there was silence. No one seemed to need leadership or direction on Friday nights. Beck didn't know what to do with himself. He tried to relax by watching television, but would turn it off within minutes because he felt that he needed to be leading people. Without people around, he felt insignificant.

His involvement in formal activities, clubs, and organizations was what he knew best. Planned involvement was all he knew. When alone on Friday nights, Beck experienced symptoms of withdrawal from organized activities. As he waited anxiously by the phone for someone to call, his body tensed up and his stomach churned. He couldn't sleep. When this occurred, Beck knew how to temporarily medicate himself: He opened his shiny black scheduler—his constant companion—to combat his involvement withdrawals. After turning just a few pages, he could easily measure his accomplishments. "Look at all I do. This campus wouldn't run without me. I'm important," he reminded himself.

One day, while quickly opening letters in his student government office, Beck noticed a nondescript letter. Unlike the other letters he opened, this letter wasn't emblazoned with a logo of a school group, club, or volunteer organization. He hoped it might be a letter from an old friend from high school. Beck received plenty of thank-you cards from organizations, but never a personal letter from an old friend. It read:

> *I know what you're going through. In a short letter, please briefly explain the details of your particular situation. I can help you.*
> *In care,*
> *DB*

He read the letter several times. He didn't know how to respond. No one ever asked Beck about himself. He thought, "What did this person DB mean by 'explain the details of your particular situation?'" Surprising even himself, he grew increasingly angry and agitated. "Explain my situation? I am Shadow U. I'm in every organization and involved in every activity on campus. People need me. People call me. When there's a problem, when there's something that needs to be accomplished, they come to me! Who would be so arrogant as to ask such a question?" he mused in disbelief. He reread the letter to make sure he had read it correctly. Each reading evoked further disgust.

A week passed without Beck responding to the letter, but he couldn't get the letter out of his head. He was outraged that somebody didn't know him. He couldn't contain himself. He cursed and yelled. Nobody knew this side of him. In public, in committee after committee, in leadership position after leadership position, Beck was composed and patient. He never lost his temper. "That wouldn't be 'leader-like,'" he rationalized.

Finally, in private, Beck broke down. He couldn't handle it anymore. His growing anger provoked him to write back to the address listed on the letter.

Dear DB,

How could you not know me? Who are you to believe you can help me? I don't need help. I help others. I'm involved in almost every club and organization on campus. I'm the president of more councils than you can imagine. I volunteer endless hours of my time to others. I don't need help. I think you've got the wrong guy.

Beck

He received DB's response six days later. He quickly opened the envelope. Inside was a letter that read:

> *Dear Beck,*
> *Thank you for your response. I'd still like to meet with you,*
> *but I know it will be difficult because of your busy schedule.*
> *I'm banned from campus, so we will have to meet at the*
> *public park across from the president's office. Meet me at*
> *3:00 p.m. on the 15th. I ask two things of you before we*
> *meet: Please bring your résumé and calendar book. Don't*
> *come unless you bring both of these very important items.*
> *And, please come alone. I look forward to meeting you.*
> *In care,*
> *DB*

Beck decided to meet DB. At the very least, Beck believed that once DB saw his extensive résumé and calendar book he would come to know that Beck didn't need any help. Beck was also curious why this person was banned from campus. "Perhaps this DB person needs my help," Beck thought.

As usual, Beck arrived five minutes early. He used the extra five minutes to review his résumé and calendar book. "Everyone's impressed when they look at my résumé," he proudly asserted to himself. Beck comforted himself, knowing that he could always point to what he did and who he was at Shadow U to prove to this person DB how important he was.

"I'm glad you showed up, Beck."

A bit shocked, Beck's eyes quickly moved from his résumé toward the voice.

"Uh…hi, you must be DB?" Still a bit leery, Beck asked, "How did you know it was me?"

"Simple. Just look around."

For the first time, Beck looked at his surroundings and noticed countless other college students talking and relaxing. Still confused, Beck shot back, "Yeah, so, that doesn't answer my question. How did you know it was me?"

"Look closer. You're the only one here looking at yourself."

"Looking at myself?"

"Yes, you're looking at yourself in your social mirror. You're so engrossed in yourself that you haven't noticed anything around you."

"My social mirror?"

"The résumé and calendar book that you were so intently examining when I approached is the sum of your identity. Some people spend hours looking at themselves in a mirror, examining the imperfections of their bodies and faces."

"I don't know what you're talking about, but I know this: if I'm looking in my social mirror, I look damn good. Who are you again and what makes you an expert?"

"Your bloated résumé and calendar book is your mirror—your social mirror. You look for your imperfections in your résumé and calendar book. I bet you when your calendar book is empty, your self-worth deteriorates."

Beck's face contorted as he thought DB was making fun of him.

Beck responded, "I don't need this. You don't know who I am. I'm not like these other people. Don't you get it?"

DB said, "I know you're well known on campus. You've been in the school newspaper almost every week. In spite of your fame, I must say one thing to you before we talk any further. Beck, you won't like this, but you're what I call a 'belongaholic.'"

"I'm not a drunk. You don't know who I am. I'm actually the president of the Student Alliance Against Binge Drinking!"

"Belongaholic, not alcoholic, Beck."

"Belongaholic?"

"From an early age, I'm sure you've been encouraged to say 'yes' to other people. I'm sure you've been told that saying 'yes' leads only to good things like recognition, awards, and achievement. I'm sure your parents told you this, your peers told you this, everyone has told you this, and you continue to tell yourself this. In your mind, organized participation equals significance."

"People look up to me; they ask for my help because they know I'm a leader. That's why I do what I do. No one's ever accused me of what you're accusing me of."

"Beck, I'm sure you're right. Organized participation is the sustenance of college life. But, when taken to an extreme, you starve yourself of the other essential aspects of the college experience."

"If I'm starving, why do so many people know who I am? Why do so many people want me to lead their clubs and organizations? Why do so many people admire me?"

"Many people with belongaholism are highly respected and thought to be healthy and normally functioning people."

"Like I said, I have no problem."

"Beck, denial is a powerful barrier to protect yourself from your belonging problem."

"Denial? You're in denial. I'm not in denial!"

"Do you mind if I take a look at your résumé?"

Reluctantly, but with pride, Beck handed his life over to him. "Bet you've never seen a résumé like that before."

"Yes, yes, very impressive," DB mumbled under his breath barely loud enough for Beck to overhear. "Just as I thought. A classic case. Your résumé proves to me that, like a good belongaholic, you only know how to say 'yes.' You're only a product of what others ask, expect, and demand of you." He returned Beck's résumé and asked, "When was the last time you thoughtfully declined an opportunity to participate?"

Stumbling, Beck could only manage to mumble, "You mean leadership opportunities? I've never said 'no' to being a leader—that's not what leaders do."

"Exactly my point. Your belongaholism is of no concern to others. Few will tell you to stop your belongaholism because your intoxication is to their benefit. The more intoxicated you become by saying 'yes' to others' requests, the less they have to do, and the less they value your participation."

"I'm a giver. I help people. What's wrong with that?"

"You do help people. Being involved is important for you and others. The problem is that you always say 'yes' to everyone and everything. You have never said 'no' to anybody, besides yourself, of course."

"If you haven't noticed, saying 'no' doesn't get you recognized in college. There's nothing strategic about saying 'no.'"

Nodding in resignation, DB stated, "When you say 'yes' to everyone—when you don't discriminate among the things to which you commit your time and efforts—you will inevitably go from participating to being used."

Confused, Beck said, "Used?"

"Yes, Beck, 'used.' People use you because you're so willing to do everything and anything. And you use yourself because you need others in order to feel important. I bet you can't control how much you participate."

"What do you mean?"

"When you always say 'yes' to others, you don't leave yourself much time to figure yourself out. You don't get publicly recognized for introspection, but it's necessary to help you understand what opportunities are worthy of saying 'yes' to and what opportunities are worthy of saying 'no' to. If you always say 'yes' to public opportunities, you'll end up gulping participation like an alcoholic does drinks."

"Why do you still think I'm an alcoholic? How many times do I have to tell you I'm not?"

"Can you stop belonging without a struggle after having just one or two club meetings?"

"I prefer my schedule filled up. Free time kills!"

"Free time kills?"

"I feel like I'm not going anywhere when I'm not participating or leading something."

"Are you saying you don't feel significant unless you're around people?"

"Significant?"

"Any withdrawal symptoms?"

"Significance? Withdrawal? Are you sure you're not the alcoholic?"

"What do you feel like when you're not in a club meeting or leading an organization?"

"That doesn't happen. I don't let it—I mean—I get involved in something immediately."

"Sounds like you suffer from a very common symptom. People who develop your symptoms generally medicate themselves by belonging more and more."

"Wait a second, are you saying I have an addiction to belonging? That's impossible. You can't be addicted to something good."

"Beck, bread is healthy, right?"

"Yeah."

"Bread is an essential part of a healthy diet. But, if you eat too much bread, it can become a poison. When taken to an extreme, anything good—whether it's bread or participation—can become unhealthy at the cost of other forms of sustenance."

"I still don't understand how someone can be addicted to participation."

"The more participation you consume, the more tolerance you develop. Eventually, you develop such an amazing tolerance that the only way you can get a social buzz is to increase your participation in organized social activities."

"You didn't answer my question, DB. Are you saying I'm addicted to belonging?"

"Unlike most students who limit their participation to what they like and enjoy doing, you feel like you *have* to be involved. You no longer choose to participate."

"DB, you're avoiding my questions."

"Sorry, Beck. You aren't as much addicted to belonging as you are addicted to acceptance. Organized participation is the clearest way to acceptance. As you said yourself, you feel important when you're leading others."

"I still don't know what the problem is. I get rewarded for my participation and leadership."

"No doubt about it. You're well known and highly respected here at Shadow U. Everyone knows about your exploits, even me. But once you help solve a group problem, once you help an organization revise its constitution, what happens?"

"We move on to the next problem."

"You feel like you're needed, right?"

"Feel? I know."

"I don't doubt that at all, Beck. When you're needed, there must be a problem; there must be something to overcome. Your belongaholic tendencies mean that people see you as needed. You don't allow others to simply hang out with you because you have convinced yourself and them that you are *only* a leader, only a fixer of problems. Sometimes, Beck, people don't need a reason to be with others. They just enjoy their company. Who do you lead on Friday nights?"

"Huh? People don't call me on Friday or Saturday nights. No big deal though…. Are you saying no one calls me on the weekends because they don't have a problem?"

"Beck, you're on the right track. Anybody who has belongaholism needs to admit they have a problem. Once you admit that participation doesn't always equal significance, you can begin to let go of the reasons that once supported your indulgence in belonging."

"Why hasn't anyone said this to me before?"

"The best person to intervene is a belongaholic."

"You're a belongaholic? Is that why you were banned from campus?"

"This is about you, Beck, not me, but remember, you're not alone in your belongaholism."

"DB, why did you want to meet with me alone? That's a little weird."

"There's no ideal time or place for a confrontation. However, you don't confront a belongaholic when he is in the midst of belonging. I picked a time and place when I knew you would be sober: a park bench outside by yourself."

"What did you do when you were a belongaholic? Are you in recovery?"

"Beck, you need a one-step program. I want you to start your own club. A very important club."

Beck thought, "Is DB now trying to trick me? Is this a game?"

Beck shot back, "You're saying someone who has belongaholism needs to start their own club? You've been drinking haven't you, DB. You're all over the place."

"Given that your entire life has been devoted to belonging and participating, I want you to use your habits to your advantage. Beck, this club has room for just one member. It will consist of you, and just you. You'll be both leader and follower. You can never cancel your scheduled meetings. You would never let others down, so now do the same for yourself. Never cancel and never be late. There's no membership fee, only a willingness to be temporarily sober. Think of it as your personal rehabilitation program."

While Beck was trying to figure out how a person could meet with himself, DB added, "Now I need something else from you."

"I've already given you enough of my time. I'm late for a meeting."

"Can I see your résumé again?"

"Will this shut you up? I'm serious, I have to go soon. Let's make this quick. Here's my résumé but it doesn't include everything. I'm not handing over my PDA—that's my life!"

"Thanks, Beck. I'm an avid recycler. This type of paper is perfect. I get top-dollar at the local recycling center."

"But…" interjected Beck.

"Don't worry. I want you to create another résumé in addition to the one you normally use. This time, devote as much effort to recounting what you strategically said 'no' to as to what you said 'yes' to. Your current résumé speaks only of what you have said 'yes' to. I'm amazed at how many activities, clubs, and organizations a person can be a part of. Very impressive résumé, Beck. As much as your diligence and energy level are impressive, I still don't know much about you from your résumé."

"Everyone's always impressed with my résumé."

"No doubt, Beck. They're initially impressed with everything you've said 'yes' to. But you don't reveal much about your character if all you do is say 'yes,' 'yes,' and 'yes!' I want you to create a résumé on which you put down what organizations and clubs you joined and led, but this time, you also have to put down on your résumé the organizations and clubs you decided not to join and lead."

"DB, when was the last time you said 'no' to anything?"

"Beck, listing both the activities you say 'yes' and 'no' to is the first step in showing others and yourself that you make choices—that you actually care about what you say 'yes' to."

"Advertising what you don't do doesn't make any sense. That's like telling people what you failed at," Beck said in a mocking tone.

"If you only list everything you say 'yes' to, that only shows you aren't very discerning."

Beck interrupted DB, "You haven't answered my question. When's the last time you said 'no' to an opportunity?"

"By learning to strategically say 'no,' you'll demonstrate purpose behind your participation and belonging. For belongaholics like us, only when we strategically say 'no' to others can we begin saying 'yes' to ourselves."

"You still haven't answered my question about what you've said 'no' to. You haven't taken your own advice, because no one in their right mind would."

"Beck, I understand how odd this sounds, but having said 'no' to Shadow U is the reason I'm here today. I can't get into the details of why, but there will be an appropriate time and place for that later."

"Lucky me. Am I somehow necessary to your recovery?"

"Beck, I'm not advocating you say 'no' for the sake of saying 'no.' I want you to start thinking about why you say 'yes' to certain opportunities. One more thing, when you begin saying 'no' thoughtfully, you'll find that other people won't even believe you at first because they're so accustomed to you saying 'yes.'"

"DB, I have to go. I'm late for a meeting."

"Beck, is it a meeting for yourself or someone else?"

"Seriously, I'm late. See ya."

While Beck hurriedly ran to his scheduled meeting, he wanted to dismiss DB's final comments. Yet he contemplated what he might do if he thoughtfully declined opportunities he had habitually said "yes" to.

Potentializer Paula

"People often prefer the certainty of pain over
an unknown future."

A million thoughts ran through Paula's head as she sat on her bed in her new dorm room surrounded by a few old possessions that had been scattered about to mask the strangeness of her new life. She had an hour to spare before the first social function of orientation week. While her favorite music played in the background, she couldn't help but think: "What have I done? Did I make the right decision? I can't believe I'm actually here."

She calmed herself with thoughts of her sister. "If Natalie did it, so can I. Look at her now; she's such an adult." Paula's sister Natalie had graduated from Shadow U the previous year. Not only did Natalie find a life partner in college, she also found something just as important: a career. Less than three months after graduation, Natalie got married, moved, and began a new career in San Francisco.

In the first awkward weeks of school, Paula did what most students do: bought books, settled into class, and made new friends. Paula had five classes. Biology was her favorite. In the third week of biology class, she met Anthony, a senior who had put off biology until his last year. Her professor randomly assigned them to the same lab group. At the time, they had no idea what a perfect match they would make. Anthony became queasy just talking about the slicing and dicing required for lab assignments, while Paula loved the hands-on experimentation of lab work. So they compromised. Paula did the slicing and dicing, while Anthony wrote up the final lab reports. After their final experiment and lab test of the semester, Paula asked Anthony out for dinner to celebrate their successful completion of biology class.

Paula looked forward to the date. She wore her favorite outfit and took extra time with her makeup. She asked her roommate for advice on which shoes to wear. In response, her roommate jokingly said, "Girl, you must really think this guy is special. You're going all out."

"Yeah, I'm excited. If biology class is any indication, there's something about Anthony that makes me want to meet him outside of class. I have a good feeling about him. At the very least, I want to give it a chance. My sister met her husband in her biology lab, so who knows?"

*　　　　　　　*　　　　　　　*

Over dinner, Anthony and Paula talked endlessly. They joked about people in their biology class. The two laughed as they told and retold stories of failed experiments and inside jokes that only two people who had worked together all semester would find funny. When they had exhausted shared classroom experiences, they turned to topics beyond class.

"Anthony, what did you do last summer?"

Anthony took a minute to respond because the question evoked more than just a simple answer. Paula didn't know it at the time, but her innocent interest in Anthony's summer touched upon an experience that had fundamentally altered his life.

"Anthony?"

"Oh, yeah…about last summer. Last summer, I interned for a political campaign. It was awesome. I actually got to work with the candidate. She gave me lots of control, and by the end of the summer, I was virtually running the campaign. I see myself working in politics when I get out of college. I can't get enough of politics."

"I love people with passion and purpose," she thought. "How sexy!"

The topic of conversation quickly moved to politics. Anthony proudly proclaimed he was a Democrat.

"So am I!" she said excitedly.

"What kind of food do you like?" he inquired.

"Japanese. I loooove Japanese food. I can't get enough. Have you been to the new Japanese restaurant near campus?"

"No, not yet, but I walk by it every day. I've wanted to eat there since it opened, but I haven't found anyone who wants to go with me. Japanese steakhouses are my favorite."

As they each ordered dessert, Paula started to think about how much they had in common.

"Paula, what type of music do you enjoy?"

"I won't tell you—you'll laugh at me. My tastes are…weird."

"Come on. Be brave. I won't laugh."

"Okay. I'm really into hip hop."

"That's cool," he shot back.

"And country!" She laughed at herself, recognizing how awkward the combination must sound.

Anthony's eyebrows raised and his eyes widened, but he didn't laugh. "Wow! That's an unusual combination. Okay, since you shared a secret with me, I'll share a secret with you that I haven't told any of my buddies. I like folk music!"

She laughed in relief at their honesty. "He didn't make fun of me," she thought. "He understands. He's funny. He's sensitive."

To make sure he knew the wave of positive energy she was experiencing, she told him, "Anthony, you make me laugh."

"Good, I like making you laugh. You have a wonderful smile."

She blushed as her smile widened.

Within hours, they had formed a connection neither could have anticipated nor imagined. In a matter of hours, they went from lab partners to intimate confidants. Ironically, the more they talked to each other, the more they listened to their internal voice instead of what their date was saying.

Paula's thoughts ran wild. "I've never met a guy like this. I've never felt so comfortable around someone so quickly." She began marking off the "perfect guy" attributes on her mental checklist.

Out of nowhere, Anthony blurted, "You know, I'm thinking of interning for her again?"

"What?"

"The candidate I worked for last summer."

"Oh, really?"

"She's unbelievable. Even though she just won the state house seat, she told me she has her eyes set on U.S. Congress. If I do a good job and she does become a congresswoman, I could work on her political staff. That would be my dream job. If I work hard and play my cards right, I could become her political advisor."

"I like his bravado," she thought. "He definitely has confidence and purpose—a must. Check."

"You know Paula, if I get this job, I will have it made—forever."

She told herself, "Job security. He has goals. He will be a great provider. Check."

"Can you imagine me as a political advisor for a congresswoman?"

Paula didn't hear him. She was preoccupied. "You said you were a Democrat, right?"

"Yeah, why?"

"Oh, just checking." She returned to her internal voice: "He's cut from the same political cloth. Necessary similarities. Check."

"Paula, I get this feeling that you're thinking about something else."

With a reassuring smile, she said, "Oh no, not at all."

As Anthony was speaking, Paula couldn't deny that she was reaching the same conclusion over and over: "Anthony is the one. He is the *right* one!" As premature as she knew it was—"This is crazy," she thought, "We've only gone out once"—she couldn't stop herself from thinking about the strangest things—her wedding, their wedding.

As speculative as he knew it was—Anthony thought, "I don't even have my dream job yet"—he couldn't resist imagining himself taking late night calls from aspiring congressional candidates in his role as acclaimed political advisor.

Picking up on the idea that Anthony might be distracted, Paula hesitantly inquired, "Are you okay?"

He responded assuredly, "Sure, yeah, of course. Everything is great."

They talked to each other and listened to their internal voices until the restaurant closed. Because Paula was so excited about the prospect of her present company being forever company, the volume on her internal voice drowned out what Anthony was saying. Because Anthony was so excited about the prospects of his internship becoming a dream job, the volume of his internal voice drowned out what Paula was saying.

It was nearly midnight when they finally left. Anthony walked Paula to her dorm room. With her lips aching for his, she fitted her body between the door and him, spun around, clasped his hands, and waited for a kiss.

"I had a great time with you tonight," he said.

She heard: "I want to be with you forever."

Before she could continue dreaming, he clasped her cheeks with his hands, stared into her eyes, smiled, and kissed her on the lips.

*   *   *

In the months that followed, Paula and Anthony did everything together. Side by side, they talked, read, wrote, studied, and shopped. They were inseparable.

They took weekend trips together, exploring life as a couple, making memories, and taking pictures of their journeys off the beaten path. On their trips, they often talked about marriage, where they wanted to live, the kind of house they wanted to live in, how many kids they wanted, what they would name their children, and what kind of parents they would be. On their trips, they also talked about Anthony's dream job: what he would be doing, how famous he would be, how much money he might make, how much influence he might wield. Whenever they talked about marriage and kids, they felt closer. Whenever they talked about Anthony's dream job, they felt closer.

Since Anthony was an avid photographer, he always developed their couple pictures. He loved mailing the pictures to Paula. The mailing wasn't necessary, since they only lived a few blocks from one another; it was just something they liked to do. It was a tradition they created and maintained together. They were both old-fashioned this way. They liked the effort of mailing letters and photographs and the anticipation of receiving mail from the one they loved. When Paula received pictures in the mail, she would stop whatever she was doing, open the package, and flip through their pictures.

Paula placed her favorite pictures on her mirror. The rest she tossed into her keepsake box. One particular day, along with a package from Anthony, she received a letter in a plain, white envelope. The letter was addressed to her. The name on the envelope had no last name, simply the initials DB with an address she didn't recognize. At the time, she thought it was junk mail, so she didn't think twice about pushing it aside as she focused on the latest package she'd received from Anthony. After picking through the pictures to determine which new photos would adorn her mirror, she put the extra pictures in her keepsake box. She didn't realize that when she put the extra pictures in her keepsake box, DB's letter got mixed up with the photos.

*   *   *

As graduation loomed, Anthony became more and more nervous. His close friends had their jobs lined up, but he had yet to receive confirmation of whether he had received his dream job. Whether right or wrong, he believed that unless he secured his dream job, he'd be unsatisfied with his other significant commitment—his relationship with Paula. He loved Paula but understood himself well enough to know he couldn't continue his relationship with her until and unless he secured the perfect job.

Anthony couldn't handle the pressure any longer. He called Paula. Their phone conversation began the same way it always did with him saying: "Hey baby. How are you?"

She had been waiting by the phone, hoping he might call. She had thought about going to dinner, but decided to eat in just in case he might call. "I'm doing great. I was thinking about you today. In fact, I dreamed about you—I mean, us—last night."

"Oh, really, what did you dream about?"

"I dreamed about us—our kids. Do you want to know the names I picked out for our beautiful kids?"

"Uh…sure, but before you do that, I have to tell you something."

She interrupted him before he could finish. "Don't worry. You don't have to like these names!"

Things were getting more difficult by the moment. He had to tell her, but she was making it almost impossible. She kept going on and on about the future. His mind wandered, wondering how he was going to tell her. He thought to himself, "I'm not just breaking up with Paula; now I have to break up with our kids." Then he caught himself: "Wait, what the…! We don't have kids. We aren't married. What's going on?" He couldn't hold back anymore. "Things are changing," he blurted. "I'm just not ready for all this responsibility."

Totally caught off guard, Paula didn't have the words to express what she was feeling: "What are you talking about, Anthony?"

Their conversation quickly turned ugly. They wrangled for almost an hour, each talking past the other. Bitterness flew from their tongues. She called him selfish, while he defensively said, "You just don't understand."

"You're right," she yelled back. "I don't understand you."

"Look, Paula, I have to get my career stuff straightened out before I make any further commitments. I have to do this first, okay?"

"Anthony, we have so much. My friends said we were perfect for each other. You said we were perfect for each other. I know we're perfect for each other. You're so selfish. You're throwing our future away in the name of a job. How could you do this to me? I counted on you to be the one. What about marriage? What about our kids? What about our future? Now that's all gone. You betrayed us."

Whether right or wrong, one thing was abundantly clear: their relationship was over. Paula was devastated. Just as confident as she had been about being with Anthony forever, she now was as certain that she would spend the rest of her life alone. Thoughts of loss overwhelmed her so much that she didn't feel like eating much. In her first two weeks without Anthony, she lost five pounds. Her friends became so worried they brought her food and made sure she ate something before they left.

Her bed became her refuge as she endlessly thought, "Life is so unfair. Why is this happening to me? Why, why, why?"

She wanted answers. She needed answers. Any answers about her future would be better than not knowing anything. Paula felt better when she told herself, "I'm okay spending the rest of my life alone. I'm okay with that. I had my time. Some people are just lucky enough to have a long-lasting relationship. Obviously, I'm not one of them."

She spent most of her waking hours thinking about Anthony and their planned life together. Thoughts of their obliterated future made her pain and loss even more difficult to bear.

Everywhere she looked she saw love—except in her life. Songs on the radio and on her iPod reminded her that, unlike the rest of the world, she didn't have anyone to share her hopes and frustrations with, no one to care about, and no one to experience life with.

Paula couldn't imagine herself with anyone besides Anthony. In a moment of sadness, she returned to her pictures. She had a bittersweet relationship with their couple pictures. They reminded her of what a great time she and Anthony used to have. At the same time, when she looked at their pictures, she was tortured by what could have been and what should have been. While Paula was looking through the photos in her keepsake box, she noticed something odd. Mixed with her pictures was a white envelope with the name DB handwritten on the front. She didn't recognize the address. She decided to open it out of curiosity. The mysterious letter read:

> I don't know you, but I know what you're going through.
> In a short letter, please briefly explain the details of your particular situation. I can help.
> In care,
> DB

The letter disturbed her. She didn't know what to think. "Who is this person? Why would somebody send me this letter?" She then looked at her watch and realized she was late. She had reluctantly promised to meet her friend, Rebecca, for coffee at 8 p.m. Paula didn't want to spend time with anyone after her breakup with Anthony, but Rebecca was adamant about making sure Paula was doing okay. Rebecca was a fifth-year senior who was a good friend of Paula's sister, Natalie. Over the years, Paula and Rebecca had become close.

After giving each other a hug, Rebecca said, "Things aren't going well, are they? It looks like you've been crying."

"I haven't talked to Anthony since we broke up. It's been weeks. We used to talk more than once a day. Every time someone calls, I think it's him. I can't stand not knowing what he's doing and if he misses me as much as I miss him. I keep looking at all of our pictures and all I can do is cry. Anthony used to send me pictures of us, when we were happy and in love. I don't get anything in the mail anymore—besides junk mail from people without last names."

"Paula, are you sure you're okay? What are you talking about?"

"Before I came out to meet you, I was looking through my keepsake box and I came across this strange letter from someone named DB."

"What's the name again?"

"Someone with the initials DB. Whoever wrote the letter said they don't know me, but understand what I'm going through. How can someone who doesn't know me understand what I'm going through? It makes no sense."

"I think I've heard of him."

"Who? It's a him?"

"If it's the same guy—then again, how many people go by the name DB and have no last name—the rumor is he worked for the Shadow U Health Center years ago but was fired. Nobody knows why he was fired, but there are plenty of rumors."

"Rebecca, why would someone from the Shadow U Health Center write me a letter?"

"Supposedly, he has this really out-there conception of what it means to be healthy while in college. He doesn't help people with broken arms or even the flu or any kind of normal sicknesses for that matter. Even though he was fired, he still helps Shadow U students."

"He's a medical doctor?"

"I'm not sure."

"But you said he worked for the Health Center?"

"That's all I've heard."

"I still don't know why he would send me a letter. Natalie never mentioned anything about a guy named DB."

"Like I said, I've only heard rumors. I've never seen him myself. Do you think there's any harm in writing him back? Maybe you should write him just to see if he'll respond."

"The letter was postmarked over a month ago."

"It's worth a shot, isn't it? You don't have anything to lose."

*　　　　*　　　　*

Paula wrote a letter to DB. She felt she couldn't pass up this opportunity. "Maybe I was meant to get a letter from DB," she thought. "Perhaps it was fate?"

Dear DB,
My boyfriend recently broke up with me. The last few
weeks of my life have been terrible. He was the one.
Without him, I feel as if I'll be alone forever.
Sincerely,
Paula

A week had passed without a response. Paula gave up on her hopes of an answer. "That only happens to people in the movies," she thought. "No one waits around this long for a response." Two weeks later, she received a letter from DB. Her spirits and hopes were rekindled.

Dear Paula,
I would still like to meet you. I can't meet on campus, so
we'll have to meet at the public park across from Shadow
U. Let's meet next Friday at 3 p.m.
I look forward to meeting you.
In care,
DB

Paula followed DB's request and waited for him at a bench in the park. By 3 p.m. Paula was getting more and more nervous by the minute as she thought about the fact that she was meeting an anonymous man in a park.

"Hi, Paula, nice to see you."

"You too," Paula said reluctantly.

"I know this is a bit awkward, but we might as well jump right in. We'll both feel more comfortable soon enough. I'm sure we have a lot to talk about."

"We do?"

"In your letter you said that your boyfriend broke up with you. Did you think you were going to spend the rest of your life with him?"

"Think? I thought I knew! We had it all figured out. We were the perfect couple. Everyone was jealous of our relationship. We talked about what our house would look like. We even knew the names of our children."

"What's his name?"

"The children?"

"No, your former boyfriend."

"Oh, Anthony."

"Let me get this straight. You thought you were going to spend the rest of your life with Anthony, and now, since he broke up with you, you're convinced you will spend the rest of your life alone. Is that right?"

"Everything we had, everything I had, disappeared in one phone call. Everything we were, everything I am, everything we shared together—gone in a matter of minutes."

"Paula, this is going to sound a little awkward at first and will take time to explain, but it's safe to say you're what I call a 'perfect potentializer.'"

"What?"

"A perfect potentializer."

Interrupting DB, Paula asserted, "I never said I was perfect."

"Let me explain. Let's start with your first date with Anthony. Take me back to when you first went out."

"We met for dinner and talked. Why?"

"What did you talk about?"

"At first, mostly about school. Then we talked about music, food, politics, you know, stuff that people talk about when they're getting to know each other."

"When you two were getting to know each other, were you talking to him while also having a conversation with yourself in your head?"

"A conversation with myself?"

"Yes, a conversation with yourself while you were having a conversation with Anthony."

"Everyone does that."

"What was the voice in your head saying?"

"It's actually pretty embarrassing."

"Try me."

"I had this little checklist thing in my head to help me determine whether he was, you know, the right one."

"As I imagined. You had a conversation with yourself to determine who Anthony could potentially be, five, ten, twenty years down the road. I bet you didn't stop there. You probably threw yourself in the mix as well, imagining who you two could potentially be together."

"So?"

"Paula, did you hear wedding bells that night?" DB asked, with a grin.

She laughed. "It's embarrassing to admit, but I did. I couldn't stop myself from planning our marriage on our first date. I knew it was weird, but I also knew I really liked him. We were laughing so much, we agreed on everything—I felt really close to him in such a short time. I must be crazy."

"Not at all. What you are is a perfect potentializer."

"I still don't get it, DB."

"Instead of thinking about who you and Anthony could potentially be, what if you had simply focused your attention on who he was right then and there?"

"I thought I was. I was paying attention to Anthony."

"Anthony, or what Anthony could become? You're not alone, Paula—we rarely pay complete attention to the person before us—most of us are perfect potentializers. It's ironic. We potentialize those people whom we feel most comfortable with, people we get along with, and people we really like. Eventually, we turn our attention away from the very person whom we like so much and spend too much of our mental energy focusing on whom they could be, what they might be able to do with us and for us."

"Are you saying I wasn't talking to Anthony on our first date?"

"You were and you weren't. Yes, you were talking to the real, physical Anthony in front of you; but you said it yourself, the loudest voice in your head was concerned with who Anthony could potentially be. The louder your inner voice talked to you about the future, the less you were interested in the real Anthony in front of you. When you were potential-izing Anthony, he became an idea that you could shape and mold into anything you wanted or needed."

"Anthony became an idea in my head? He was real. I have pictures of us to prove how much we cared for each other."

"Do you spend a lot of time these days looking at your couple pic-tures?"

"Actually, I spend more time looking at them now than I did when we were dating."

"That makes sense."

"No, it doesn't. When I look at my pictures, I mean, our pictures, I feel terrible and sometimes I cry."

"You cry because you miss Anthony?"

"Yeah, of course."

"Is it possible you're also crying and mourning over what could've been?"

"Now, I'm really confused. I miss Anthony. I get most upset looking at pictures of us together, smiling. I burst into tears when I see us smil-ing, looking so happy together. I can't get out of my head what we're missing out on together, how good we could've been together."

"When you're a perfect potentializer, and the actual, real relationship ends, it's hard to tell what you're breaking up with."

"I broke up with Anthony—I mean, he broke up with me."

"Paula, in addition to mourning the physical absence of Anthony, you're also mourning the loss of what you and Anthony might have cre-ated together. Whether we want to believe it or not, sometimes we fall in love with what could potentially be as much as with the actual person. It's a double whammy!"

"I know one thing for sure, DB—I was definitely in love with Anthony."

"That's what makes this all so difficult. Paula, where's Anthony now?"

"He graduated. That's why he supposedly broke up with me."

"What?"

"He didn't have his dream job before graduating, so he abandoned everything else until he got the job he wanted."

"Did Anthony ever talk about his dream job?"

"Yeah, he talked about it a lot, even on our first date. He told me he completed an internship for a political campaign. Anthony loves politics. He couldn't stop talking about how his internship could potentially lead to a job on the political staff of some congresswoman, even though she hadn't even been elected yet."

"Really?"

"Yeah, even though she just won a state house seat, Anthony imagined helping her get elected to U.S. Congress."

"Paula, do you notice something else that you and Anthony shared in addition to love?"

"I guess I wasn't the only perfect potentializer in the relationship."

"Paula, you said Anthony didn't secure his dream job before graduation, correct?"

"That's right."

"When Anthony talked about what he could potentially be, when you and Anthony talked about what you two could potentially be, did the future appear certain?"

"Absolutely! Like I said, for the first time, everything in my life appeared clear. At least in comparison to what I feel like now—totally lost. When I was dating Anthony, for the first time ever, I felt like I knew what I was doing. I was more confident and sure of things. Were we lying to ourselves, DB?"

"Not exactly."

"Do you ever give a clear answer?"

"Not really. Sorry, I know it can be quite annoying. Paula, you weren't lying in the traditional sense. It's more complicated than that."

Frustrated, Paula interrupted DB, "Okay, fine, if we can't avoid potentializing, then how do we know when we've gone too far?"

"That's a hard one, too. A perfect potentializer desires certainty at all costs. In fact, your desire to know what your future holds overshadows your well being. Paula, we can't help but propel ourselves into the future—even though our bodies are stuck in the present."

"I know one thing: everything I thought was going to happen didn't!"

"We feel like we have to know what our future will look like or we think we're lost. Once your relationship with Anthony ended, so did your imagined certainty about what was to come. When you were dating Anthony and perfectly potentializing, you mixed up what *could* happen with what *should* happen. Sure, you could've been with Anthony forever. That's a lot different than believing that you should be with Anthony forever. So now, when your future seems so uncertain, you convince yourself that you will be alone forever."

"The worst part is, I think about being alone forever right before I go to bed. I haven't been able to sleep much lately."

"Convincing yourself that you'll be alone forever makes you feel better. If you convince yourself that you will be alone forever, at least you have certainty. And we already agreed that you feel better when you are certain."

"I must be going crazy, DB. You're a doctor, aren't you? Maybe you can give me something to help?"

"You don't need a doctor. If anything, Paula, you're too sane. Ironically, we believe knowing what will happen to us—whether miserable or blissful—is better than not knowing. Even if you feel terrible when you convince yourself that you will be alone forever, you also find comfort in seemingly knowing your future."

"Great, thanks for reminding me of why I will live a comfortably miserable life forever!"

"Not so fast. Just because we find comfort in thinking we know the future, that doesn't mean we are always right."

"Of course not, that would be too easy," Paula said sarcastically.

"You asked a few minutes ago about how you know when you've potentialized too much. You know you've gone too far when you're held hostage by your potentializations."

"Held hostage? If my potentializations were accurate, then I'd be with Anthony right now."

"True, but what if you and Anthony grew apart? What if you both changed? What if you stopped caring about Anthony? Would you feel trapped? What if he changed? Would he feel frustrated?"

"I guess it's possible."

"You agree that your future together once appeared certain to you."

"Yeah."

"When Anthony discovered that securing his dream job was uncertain, he began to reexamine certain areas of his life, including his relationship with you. His doubts and fears about not landing his dream job overflowed into your relationship. Tell me what he said when he broke up with you."

"Something like…he needed to get his dream job situation straightened out before he could commit to anything else, including his relationship with me."

"Just as I expected."

"What?"

"He couldn't bear the burden of being uncertain about his dream job while being certain about his dream girl. He wanted certainty. He found comfort in making everything about his life uncertain. Certainty won."

"He found certainty by making everything uncertain. That doesn't seem right, DB."

"People often prefer the certainty of pain over an unknown future."

"Right now, it seems like potentializing can only lead to misery."

"Potentialization isn't in itself a bad thing. Potentialization helps us prepare for the future and provides motivation; though excessively indulging in thoughts about what could potentially be is unhealthy, because eventually you will end up being used by your potentializing."

"Then why do we do it?"

"Because we convince ourselves we have to be certain about our futures—whether terrible or fantastic, married or single, unemployed or employed. We mistakenly assume that tomorrow will look like today."

"Isn't that the way things happen?"

"Does it appear to you as if everything stays the same from one day to the next—that your life is a straight line without any curves in the road?"

"It seems pretty straight and miserable to me right now, DB!"

"I'm sure it does, Paula."

"I don't want this to happen again, DB."

"I'm sorry to have to tell you that it might."

"Then why did we spend all this time talking about potentializing if there's nothing I can do to prevent it?"

"Even though you can't prevent it, you can cure it."

"How?"

"We've already started. Before our conversation, you didn't have a way of talking about what was going on in your head. Before you met me, you couldn't separate the hurt you were feeling caused by your breakup with Anthony from the hurt caused by your potentializing."

"You're right. All I knew was that I was hurting. I still miss Anthony desperately, but I guess I was trying to get over my breakup with Anthony *and* my breakup with what Anthony and I were going to be, forever."

"Paula, do you now see how our conversation was part of the cure?"

"So the cure is in the conversation?"

"Or the conversation is in the cure."

"There you go again, DB. The cure is where?"

"Forgive me for my unconventional logic. In all seriousness, our conversation has helped you better respond to a recurring situation that typically overwhelms students in college."

"DB, how do you know so much about this stuff? Where did you come up with a term like 'potentializing?'"

"It's a long story, Paula. In many ways, I..."

"I'm sorry DB, how rude. It's my cell phone."

Paula answered her phone. "Hey, Rebecca. You're not going to believe this but...remember that letter I received from the guy named DB? I'm meeting with him now.... Hold on for a second."

"DB, it's my friend Rebecca."

"I have to get some dinner anyway. I'll let you two talk in private," DB said as he waved goodbye to Paula before she could try to convince him not to leave.

"Did you find out who he is and why he got fired?" Rebecca asked.

"That's weird...we talked for a long time, but I didn't find out anything about him. I feel like I talked the whole time."

"What did DB say about you and Anthony?"

"Anthony and I were liars."

Rebecca couldn't believe what she was hearing. "Paula, you're the most honest person I know."

"Not that kind of lying, Rebecca. We betrayed ourselves because we remained too loyal to the futures we created in our heads."

"DB said you were too loyal?"

"Pretty much. I guess I became so comfortable with what was going to happen, and what didn't happen, that I forgot that talking or thinking about the future doesn't make it any more real."

Students Who Binge Together, Stay Together

"Conversation cures binge thinking because it exposes
the thoughts that we can't make sense of when they remain muddled
in the privacy of our own minds."

Three weeks before the end of the spring semester, DB individually contacted Anna, Beck, Paula, Tyler, and Maya. He wrote each of them the following:

> *Congratulations on making it through the school year.*
> *Before you depart for the summer, let's meet at noon on the*
> *last Saturday of the spring semester at the public park across*
> *from Shadow U. Please let me know if you can make it.*
> *I look forward to seeing you.*
> *In care,*
> *DB*

He heard from Paula and Anna within a few days. They agreed to meet.

A couple days after he received DB's letter, Beck saw DB walking into a diner near campus. He waved and said, "DB, I got your letter. I'll be there. But one thing: I might be a little late because I scheduled a meeting with myself."

"Oh…really. How are your meetings going, Beck?"

"At first, I denied my problem."

"I remember."

"It hit me hardest the Friday night following our meeting. You were right, no one called when they didn't need me for something. I was tired of feeling like being by myself was a failure."

"I still struggle with the same issues," DB said reassuringly.

Maya e-mailed DB, writing, "DB, I'm busy with my career stuff, but I can probably fit you in☺. See you soon!" The smiley face meant that she was now quite aware of her tendency to abuse the moment. Her previous e-mails had never contained a smiley face. The old Maya was too busy to have fun. DB laughed when he received her e-mail.

One more week had passed and still no word from Tyler.

"Maybe I gave Tyler too much time to respond," thought DB, half-jokingly. "Then again, if I sent the letter only a couple days before our meeting, he might say, 'Hey, you didn't give me enough time.'" Several days later, Tyler wrote back: "Sorry about my late response. I was trying to figure out which activity to drop from my schedule. If I added anything more to my workload, I would've been doing too much; but I'll make time for you, DB."

*   *   *

On that last Saturday of the spring semester, Paula, Beck, Anna, Maya, and Tyler met DB at the public park across from Shadow U. DB brought two letters. Beck brought just himself, no daily planner. Maya brought just herself as well—no career books.

"Thanks for coming, everybody," said DB.

Paula, Beck, Anna, Maya, and Tyler didn't hear DB. They were all distracted.

In a hesitant and surprised voice, Maya said, "DB, I thought it was just going to be you and me. I didn't know there would be other Shadow U students here." Everyone nodded in confused agreement. DB allowed their puzzled gazes to continue without interruption. He knew his welcoming wasn't heard. They continued to look at each other, trying to detect whether anybody looked familiar. Nobody but Beck looked familiar to them.

Pointing her finger at Beck, Anna said, "You're always in the *Shadow U Chronicle*, right?"

Before Beck could respond, Maya, an avid reader of the *Shadow U Chronicle*, said, "Yeah, I knew you looked familiar." With a hint of envy, Maya added, "Must be nice to be in the school paper."

Beck had set the Shadow U record for college newspaper appearances. Out of a hundred and twenty-eight issues over the past three years, Beck had appeared in fifty-five papers. The editors didn't even file Beck's digital photo; they kept it on their computer desktop for easy access. Beck was the only Shadow U student with this distinction.

"Easy, folks, Beck rushed a meeting with himself to be here today. So let's be kind," said DB with a smirk.

Looking around at the group, Paula said, "DB, it's nice to see that there are other perfect potentializers at Shadow U." A chorus of confusion immediately erupted. The others looked at Paula with bewildered expressions.

DB interrupted the growing furor. "Ah...my friends, why don't you introduce yourselves to the group?"

Confident she knew who she was, Paula proudly said, "Hi, my name is Paula and I'm a perfect potentializer."

Not wanting to be left out, Beck followed suit. "Hi, my name is Beck and I'm a belongaholic."

Then the others chimed in.

"Hi, my name is Tyler and I'm tortured by the too."

"Hi, my name is Anna and I'm addicted to aloneness."

"Hi, my name is Maya and I'm a moment abuser."

All five named themselves using the same language DB had used to diagnose them earlier in the school year. After their introductions, all five looked inquisitively at one another, sensing they shared something in common but weren't quite able to pinpoint what it was.

Everyone was fixated on DB, anticipating what he might say. This was the moment DB had hoped for. All five had already met with him during the school year, but DB had more to say: "I'm impressed. Given your introductions, it sounds like all of you learned a thing or two from the conversations I had with each of you during the school year."

"Yeah," they collectively answered.

"But I want to make sure all of you know that this meeting is not about you, it's about binge thinking."

"Binge *thinking*?" asked Anna.

DB then reintroduced each binge in more detail so he could explain what he meant. "Paula, you binged on the superbly creative ability to turn a first date into a relationship that would last forever. Beck, you binged on the need to belong by always saying 'yes' to others and 'no' to yourself. Anna, you binged on thoughts of aloneness by seeing yourself as different from your peers and waiting for others to tell you who you were. Tyler, you binged on dissatisfaction and saw everything in your life as too little or too much. Maya, you binged on the belief that your future was always more important than your present."

They sat quietly, reflecting on DB's observations. DB then asked, "Does anyone know why I arranged a group meeting?"

"Because there's something wrong with us, DB?"

"Anna, all of you have indulged in what I call 'binge thinking,' but binge thinking isn't about *you*."

"What do you mean binge thinking isn't about us?" inquired Beck.

"All of you are here today because you binged on your thoughts."

Before DB could continue, Paula interrupted, "How did you know I was binge thinking before we met? Why did you send me a letter—did someone tell you I was binge thinking?"

"You're not the only Shadow U students I contacted this year."

Maya still didn't have things figured out. "When you contacted me, you wrote, 'I don't know who you are, but I know what you're going through.' DB, is everyone in college a binge thinker?"

"Everybody in college habitually binges on their thoughts. I meet with lots of students every year who binge on thoughts—moment abuse, potentializing, addiction to aloneness, belongaholism, tortured by the too—just like all of you. It's not a matter of *if* you're going to binge think, it's just a question of *when*. I can talk to any Shadow U student about binge thinking because all students have indulged in binge thinking, are binge thinking, or will binge think on the mental challenges of college life. I brought you five together today because all of you happened to be in the midst of super-intense binges when we talked."

Paula wasn't following DB's logic. She asked, "I know binge drinkers get sick when they drink too much. But, how can you tell when you think too much?"

"Before I answer your question, I need someone to answer my question: why and when do you go to a doctor?"

Matter-of-factly, Beck said, "I go to a doctor when I'm sick."

"Okay, Beck, how do you know when you're sick?"

"I go when I'm not feeling right. A year ago, I was involved in so many activities and organizations that I started feeling sick. I didn't have time to slow down; so I kept going nonstop. Eventually, I couldn't even get out of bed. I was so exhausted—day and night. My throat was swollen. My joints ached. I was so bad off I had to have someone help me get to the Health Center."

DB interrupted, "And tell us what the doctor did."

"I explained my symptoms and he examined me. He then took some blood. Later that week, he called and told me I had mono."

"Perfect!"

Beck shouted, "Perfect?! I had to give up all my activities that semester—I was president of three different organizations. It was terrible!"

"I'm sorry, Beck. I meant you provided us with a perfect example. The doctor who examined you was trained to make sense out of your symptoms. After listening to your symptoms, the doctor organized them into the most logical diagnosis: mono. Then he confirmed his hypothesis with a blood test."

"What are you getting at, DB?" asked Tyler.

"Binge thinking can make you sick like binge drinking, but there's a difference—and this is an important difference: the Health Center can't diagnose you when you yourself don't even know when you're binge thinking. Remember that Beck went to the doctor because he wasn't feeling well. But why didn't all of you go to the Health Center?"

Silence followed DB's question for what seemed like minutes. Interrupting the silence, DB answered for them. "Your silence is the answer. Prior to meeting me, some of you didn't even know you were binge thinking. Even if you did know that you were binge thinking, you still wouldn't have gone to get help because you didn't have a language to explain binge thinking to yourself, let alone someone else."

"Beck, one more question about your doctor visit: Did you feel better after you went to the doctor?"

"Even though there was nothing the doctor could prescribe for mono besides rest, I felt better after I left the doctor's office because I knew *why* I wasn't feeling or acting like my normal self."

Tyler asked Beck, "What do you mean your 'normal self?'"

"After I was diagnosed with mono, I knew why I had been feeling so tired. I knew why I wasn't performing as well in my classes as I had before I got sick."

"Exactly. When Beck was diagnosed with mono, his condition was legitimized. I bet he was able to write an e-mail to his professors and boss explaining why he didn't attend his classes and show up for work. Most likely, they understood the reasons why he stayed home because they were able to publicly acknowledge and accept his condition."

"You're right, DB. After I was diagnosed with mono, people were more accepting of my condition."

"I thought we were talking about binge thinking," Maya said partly out of frustration and partly out of curiosity.

"We are, Maya. Naming your binges legitimizes your thoughts. The key is knowing when *thinking* about the mental challenges that every college student encounters—thoughts of loneliness, the desire for recognition, the need to belong, the stress of dissatisfaction, and the pressures of finding a perfect relationship and an ideal job—turns into *binge* thinking."

"I still don't understand when I went from thinking to *binge* thinking."

"In your case, Paula, you started binge thinking when you thought you were going to spend the rest of your life alone and miserable after your breakup with Anthony."

"Why don't more people know about binge thinking?"

"Maya, do you remember our conversation on IM. You weren't convinced you were binge thinking. That's because you were institutionally rewarded for abusing the moment. In the process of our conversation, I had to first draw your attention to the fact that everything you thought about and did was in preparation for the future. Moment abuse didn't miraculously appear. Moment abuse helped you gain admiration and respect from Shadow U professors and your family. Binging on moment abuse served a purpose at some point, but you took it too far—you couldn't control it. It began controlling you."

"She's not alone," Paula added.

"You're right, Paula. All Shadow U students indulge in binge thinking. Most of them, excluding all of you, don't even know it!"

"Okay, so we know when Maya and Paula began binge thinking, but what about the rest of us," asked Anna. "When did we begin binge thinking?"

Beck seconded Anna's question, "Yeah, I still don't get the difference between thinking and *binge* thinking."

"Unfortunately, binge thinking isn't as easy to detect as binge drinking."

Tyler raised his voice and shot back at DB, "There's got to be a clear-cut way to figure out when someone is binge thinking."

"All of you know that the most important things in life can't be measured. We don't go to a love expert to determine whether we're in love or not. We don't hook ourselves to a love machine to diagnose how much we're in love with someone. But, just because we can't measure love doesn't mean it doesn't exist."

"Love hurts, DB. Love hurts," Paula said as everyone erupted in laughter.

"Thinking becomes binge thinking when your binge becomes a major part of your college experience. Beck, you went from thinking to binge thinking when you became a belongaholic and needed institutional acceptance so much that you forgot how to say 'no' to others and 'yes' to yourself. Anna, you went from thinking to binge thinking when you became addicted to aloneness and became more comfortable in isolation than in the company of others and when you waited for others to tell you who you were when you knew yourself better than anyone else. Tyler, you went from thinking to binge thinking when you tortured yourself with the 'too' by interpreting things in your life as too little or too much."

"DB, where do we go for help?"

"Anna, remember, your binges are a reflection of the challenges you face in college."

"Should we drop out of college, then?"

"Anna, it's not that simple."

Maya challenged DB. "Dropping out of school makes sense to me. You said that binge thinking is encouraged in college. If we drop out of college, then we can also completely avoid binge thinking, right?"

"Maya, you're going to make a good lawyer—I mean, senator— someday. You hold me accountable for what I say. Very impressive! I had a feeling all of you would want proof on this one, so I brought a letter that I think will prove my point. I hope you don't mind if I take a few minutes and read this letter. I think it will help me explain what I'm getting at."

DB then read the letter to the group.

> *Dear Shadow U President,*
>
> *My college experience was miserable before I met DB my junior year. Let's just say college wasn't always the best time of my life as you promised us freshmen during orientation week.*
>
> *DB from the Health Center is the man! He showed me that college is a breeding ground for binge thinking. Was he ever right! After I met DB, I knew I was miserable in college because I was unprepared to handle binge thinking. Don't you know what's going on at Shadow U? Don't you care?*
>
> *I have too much respect for myself to continue harming my health. It's either college or my sanity. I'm going to quit Shadow U. I'm better off without binge thinking.*
> *Sincerely,*
> *Maddox*

DB folded the letter and put it back in his pocket, still holding onto one other letter.

"You told Maddox to quit college?"

"No, Tyler. Absolutely not. Maddox jumped to conclusions. He didn't pay attention when I tried to explain the cure for binge thinking. The president read Maddox's letter and immediately thought I had told him to quit Shadow U."

"DB, Maddox's letter mentioned that you worked at the Health Center. Is that true?"

"Paula, I used to work at the Health Center. When I tried to explain my side of the story to the president, he simply said, 'DB, I can't have you mischaracterizing the college experience. We can't have staff—especially people who work in the Health Center—encouraging students to drop out by saying that college is a breeding ground for binge thinking. I'm in the business of making sure students graduate. Either you're on board with that or you're not. I warned you once before, but obviously you didn't heed my warning. For the good of the university, I must let you go. After you leave today, don't set foot on this campus again.' Before I could respond, the president ushered me out the door."

"He fired you for one lousy letter? That's a buncha crap," said Tyler.

"I never told Maddox to transfer or quit college altogether. He made that fateful decision on his own without talking to anybody."

"Maddox was a loner?" asked Anna.

"No, Maddox just didn't know *how* to talk to anyone about his bouts of binge thinking. He stopped listening to me after he heard about binge thinking. Maddox failed to realize that binge thinking wasn't unique to Shadow U. He mistakenly thought that if he removed himself from Shadow U, he would remove himself from binge thinking. Walking away from college seems like the answer, but it's not."

Paula said, "Okay, okay. I think we accept the fact that quitting college isn't a reasonable option, but can you give us something more to help us combat binge thinking?"

"I must disclose one more thing to you—that is, one more letter. Tyler, maybe this will help you understand why the Shadow U president was so unwilling to listen to me. Maddox's letter wasn't the only letter he received that involved me. About three years before Maddox's letter, the president called me into his office. I thought he wanted to thank me for my service to Shadow U. When I arrived, he presented a copy of a letter from concerned parents of a Shadow U student."

DB still had the original letter. He read it out loud, believing it would help answer some of the group's questions.

> *Dear Shadow U President,*
>
> *During his first two years at Shadow U, our son Joey wasn't doing well. Despite having a B average, a girlfriend, and being active in campus life, something was missing. Instead of having the best time of his life, he gained weight, distanced himself from family and friends, and developed a pessimistic attitude toward life.*

As concerned parents, seeing our son this way alarmed us. We had believed that all of Joey's hard work to get into college was finally going to be rewarded. How wrong we were! The last two years were filled with a series of distressed phone calls from Joey. Most of the time, we tried to console him by telling him that everything would be all right. We reassured him on the phone, but privately we were confused and distraught. We didn't know what was happening to the Joey we once knew. And we surely didn't know how to help him help himself.

Then a friend of Joey's suggested he visit DB at the Shadow U Health Center. Joey eventually visited DB. After only a couple of visits with DB, Joey seemed like a different person. He carried himself with pride and even began laughing again with his friends. He became the Joey we knew before he went to Shadow U. It was a joy and a blessing to see our son this way. Our two years of prayers were answered. We asked Joey what medication DB had prescribed. Joey told us DB didn't give him any prescription drugs. Instead, DB taught Joey how to cure binge thinking. Joey said DB explained to him that college is a breeding ground for binge thinking that, if unaddressed, can negatively affect his well-being.

Joey told us that he started feeling better once DB helped him realize that he was not alone in binge thinking. We wanted you to know how much we appreciate DB helping our son.
Sincerely,
Mr. and Mrs. Strongross

DB folded the letter and put it in his pocket.

"DB, that sounds like a positive letter, but it doesn't explain everything. Don't you still owe me more of an explanation for when you said 'no' to others? You told me you would tell me. I think now is as good as ever."

"I thought the letter was positive too, Beck, though that isn't what the president thought. He kept reading and rereading the sentence from Joey's parents, 'college is a breeding ground for binge thinking.'"

"Why did he get so upset over that one statement?" asked Beck.

"He thought it was an indictment of his college, which in turn, was an indictment of him as president. I tried to explain that Shadow U isn't different from any other college, but he didn't want to hear it. My insights and unconventional cures threatened him. He told me then that if he received another letter like this one, he would have no recourse but to fire me. When he got Maddox's letter, I was as good as gone; but I was okay with getting fired because I believed in my cures more than I did in my job. There's the answer to your question, Beck. I strategically said 'no' to the president and said 'yes' to helping students."

Anna was still puzzled. "DB, I still don't understand how someone could believe that you were mischaracterizing the college experience. From everything I know of you, you're the last person I would accuse of misunderstanding the college experience."

"Anna, I love Shadow U; I worked for the Health Center most of my life. In all my years here, Shadow U has enrolled bright, young minds; educated them; and in many ways, prepared them for life beyond college. When I talk of binge thinking, I'm not criticizing Shadow U. It does what it sets out to do. Despite all of the good the college provides, I have always believed there's something more that can be offered to Shadow U students during their college experience."

"Hold on a minute, DB, I think you're getting off topic. You said Maddox didn't pay attention to you when you talked about the cure to binge thinking. So, what's the cure?"

"Maya, the beginning of a cure for binge thinking is learning a 'binge' vocabulary. With a binge vocabulary, you can separate binge thinking from yourself just as Beck was able to distinguish mono from himself. The doctor didn't diagnose Beck; he diagnosed mono."

"So, you didn't diagnose me; you diagnosed moment abuse?"

"Correct, Maya. And that's the case with each of you. I diagnosed your specific binge, not you personally."

Still confused, Beck asserted, "But I was sick."

"Beck, the doctor diagnosed mono, he didn't diagnose you as a person. Likewise, a binge vocabulary enables you to distinguish the binge *from* you. Binge thinking isn't a part of you as much as it is a part of the college culture. When you get the binge out of your head, you can begin to understand it separately from yourself."

"I guess you're right, DB," acknowledged Tyler. "After we talked, I felt better. For the first time, I understood what I was doing to myself. I was able to explain what was going on in my head to my parents. Before I knew what was torturing me, I felt like I was the only one on campus who was feeling the way I was—too much of this and not enough of that. I didn't bring it up with any of my friends because I didn't know what to say."

"After our talk, things changed for me, too," Paula added.

"What changed?" DB asked.

"I still miss Anthony and still wonder what he's up to. But, after our talk, I knew I was definitely in the midst of a nasty binge. Eventually, I went out on another date, and sure enough, I started to potentialize about a second date while I was still on our first date. Once I recognized I was potentializing and not listening to what my date was saying, I tried to refocus my attention on the actual person in front of me instead of the fictional person I was creating in my head."

"I guess I've changed, too."

"Really, how so, Maya?" asked DB.

"I realized that all I concerned myself with was preparing myself for something in the future. As you suggested, I tried living one week without abusing the moment. I tried to enjoy the simple things in life without worrying about how everything I did might affect my future. This is going to sound weird, but…I read a book."

"Congratulations, Maya! You can read!" Tyler yelped.

"No…I mean, yes, I can read, but I read a book for fun. I read fiction. That was the first time in college I read something that wasn't on a syllabus. And, I'm even thinking about taking a yoga class. Until my binge was diagnosed, I didn't even know how much of my life had become devoted to preparing for something in the future."

"That's quite a transformation, Maya. When students have a binge vocabulary, they can understand that their binge is not a reflection of them as much as it's a reflection of the college culture."

"Slow down, DB. Don't only sick people get diagnosed?"

"Anna, a binge vocabulary isn't for people who are sick. Everyone who goes to college will endure one or more of the binges all of you have indulged in. Too often, when students binge think, they believe there's something wrong with them, and as a result, they isolate themselves from others."

"Sort of like we quarantine ourselves?"

"Yes, I couldn't have said it better myself, Beck. If you isolate yourself when binge thinking, or, as Beck says, quarantine yourself, you only do more harm."

"That actually makes sense," replied Paula. "When I binged on potentializing, I didn't want to talk to anyone—I only wanted to listen to sad music. It's weird, but I felt better when I wasn't talking to anyone."

"Exactly! When you're in the midst of a binge like the one you were experiencing after your breakup, your first impulse is to isolate yourself. To cure binge thinking, however, you must socialize it."

"Socialize it? You've been reading too much Marx!"

"No, Beck, not socialism. Socialize it—make it public. When I met with you individually, I helped you diagnose the thinking binges you were indulging in so you could learn how to talk about them with others. Everyone in this group has experienced binge thinking at one point or another."

"All of us have binged on our thoughts? Don't you mean just us?" Anna said as she pointed at her peers.

"No, Anna, I mean *us*. Like all of you, I've binged on my thoughts, too. Who better to intervene than someone who has indulged in binge thinking?"

Everyone looked at DB in shock, except Beck.

"Wow," Tyler said. "You're just like us!"

"Yes, I am. Remember, I've been on a college campus for most of my life in one capacity or another. Binge thinking has been my constant companion throughout."

In disbelief, Anna asked DB, "How did you prevent yourself from going loco? I mean, how did you stay sane all these years?"

"Good question. Sometimes I wonder myself," he said jokingly. "I've had the advantage of being on a college campus for many years. I've noticed the same binges year after year. All of you only have four or five years in college, and I know it's hard enough just to get by with all that you're asked to do. You have to focus on your immediate circumstances—the next midterm, a final paper, getting an internship, relationships, meeting friends, making money, and building your résumé. When you have to do so much, it's hard to see how the college culture requires certain patterns of thought from everyone."

"I hate to say this, but everyone here has different binges; so we can't have that much in common."

"You're technically correct, Anna. Everyone here has indulged in different thinking binges. As college students, however, you'll always have binge thinking in common despite the minor differences that make you diverse—grades, major, senior or freshman, science or liberal arts major, ethnicity, politics, religion, and so forth."

Beck asked in disbelief, "So, all we need is a binge vocabulary to help us talk to others about binge thinking?"

"A binge vocabulary is a great start in helping you make sense of the thinking binges encouraged by the college culture. But it's not just a set of vocabulary terms."

"Good. I don't have time. You know my schedule, DB," Maya said with a grin.

"You need your own language to talk to your peers and your parents about the college experience that goes beyond the institutional vocabulary of studying and grades. Some students are proud of their grades, yet they don't tell others who don't do as well. Some students are embarrassed about their grades, so they don't tell anyone."

"Why are we talking about grades all of a sudden?" asked Tyler.

"Tyler, binge thinking defies grade point average. When you have a language to talk about binge thinking, you know you're not alone. You always have something in common with the person next to you because you know they have indulged in binge thinking, are binge thinking, or will binge think."

"I hate to be a downer, but I have to ask what's in this for you, DB? Why did you take all the time to meet with each of us individually?"

"I don't blame you, Paula. I would ask the same question if I were in your position. But the binge vocabulary works the same for me as it does for you. Over the years, I've created a binge vocabulary to help me understand and explain my bouts of binge thinking with others. All of you are medicinal for me, too. I should be giving thanks to all of you."

"We helped you, DB? I never thought of it that way," said a surprised Paula.

"Wait a second. I know what this reminds me of. I couldn't think of it earlier, but now it's coming to me. DB, our gathering today is like a support group for students enduring binge thinking. Can I add this organization to my résumé?" Beck asked.

Everyone laughed at Beck's comment, yet each knew intuitively that he was right. Without realizing it, they had formed their own recovery group, and yes, Beck really did want to be their leader.

"Where is our next BTA meeting?"

"What are you talking about now, Beck?"

"BTA—Binge Thinkers Anonymous. When is our next meeting?" Beck quickly said. "I'll be the president."

"Slow down, Beck. Before you begin organizing our first meeting, I must make an amendment to BTA."

"What amendment, DB? I'm really good at writing club constitutions, so this should be no problem."

"If everyone in college binge thinks at some point, then it shouldn't be anonymous. As we all know now, if you keep your bouts of binge thinking private, you're in real trouble because you have no way of talking about it with others. When you talk about binge thinking with others, you can understand what you're experiencing, find acceptance from others, and even laugh at the binges."

"Yeah, I'm sure some of my friends would love to know how to cure binge thinking," said Paula.

"Maybe you can teach them what you know," said Maya.

"Yeah, maybe," said Paula, hesitantly.

"Don't ever underestimate the healing power of thoughtful conversation," said DB.

"It definitely helped me," assured Paula.

"Conversation cures binge thinking because it exposes the thoughts that we can't make sense of when they remain muddled in the privacy of our own minds. Only when you talk about binge thinking in the company of others can you transcend binge thinking and poke fun at the binges—not yourself. On the other hand, when you isolate yourself in the midst of binge thinking, the binges only intensify and can go beyond your control. You're all more than ready. Go share with your friends what I shared with you. They will love you for it; you'll find they share many of the same binges you do. Just be careful—you know what they say?" DB added.

"What?" asked Paula.

"Students who binge together, stay together," exclaimed DB with a grin.

Everyone erupted in laughter.

"Have you noticed that everyone is laughing about binge thinking—and not themselves?"

"You're right, DB. I thought this meeting was going to be a bummer," said Tyler. "I thought for sure there would be too much seriousness."

DB asked, "What's different, Tyler?"

"It's fun to laugh at the binge rather than yourself! It's cool knowing it's not personal. Hey…Where are you going, DB? This is just starting to get good."

"I have to go, Tyler. I have another meeting with other Shadow U students. I'll see you all again soon."

They waved goodbye and continued to share stories about the binges they had never before shared. The more they talked, the louder they laughed, and the more fun they had.

Pretending to get up to leave, Paula said, "Hey, guys, gotta go—I just met this guy today at lunch, and I need to pick out our wedding invitations."

Following Paula's lead, Anna said, "I should leave, too. I need to go to a basketball game so I can find 15,000 reasons not to talk with any of the fans in the arena! It's a great talent. Anyone want to join me?"

"Beck, you a little lost without your résumé?" quipped Tyler.

"Uh…Tyler, be careful now, you might be trying tooooo hard to be funny. Plus, are you sure you got yourself enough to do this summer, hmmm?" countered Beck.

In a mock-stern voice, Maya quipped, "Settle down, everyone—do you know who's in your presence? A lawyer—I mean, a distinguished senator. Quiet down now, you should treat me with the respect I deserve!"

These Shadow U students who once privately binged on thoughts of loneliness, the desire for recognition, the stress of dissatisfaction, the need to belong, and the pressure to obtain a perfect relationship, now laughed together at the very binge thinking that previously consumed them.

Dear College Students,

Please share your binge thinking experiences with me at dbfreeme@borgesandwhite.com. Was your binge like Tyler's, Maya's, Paula's, Beck's, or Anna's? If so, share your binge thinking experience. Or do you have a different kind of thinking binge to share? If so, please share the binge and, of course, what you've named it. With your permission, I'd like to post your story and thoughts so others can learn and be inspired!

Also, if you're a musician, author, artist, photographer, film producer, painter, web junkie, or have any talent for transforming binge thinking into meaningful art, please consider being selected for my "best of binge" art series. Currently, I'm collecting binge art and will select the best submissions to be featured in future binge books, galleries, music labels, and photographs. If you'd like to be considered, please submit your materials and contact information to this address:

DB
P.O. Box 318
Fernley, NV 89408

If you need a gift for yourself or a fellow binger, visit borgesandwhite.com for the most recent "Binge Thinking" gifts. Remember, publicizing binge thinking is an important step in curing binge thinking!

In care,
DB

Dear Parents of College Students,

Just like every parent, you want your child to have the best college experience possible. That's why, as the caring parent you are, you took the first step by reading *Binge Thinking*. You know that your investment wouldn't be complete unless you are able to meaningfully understand and talk about the binges your child endures during their college experience.

As a parent of a college student, please share your child's binge thinking experiences by e-mailing me at dbfreeme@borgesandwhite.com. Was your child's thinking binge like Tyler's, Maya's, Paula's, Beck's, or Anna's? Or did they experience a different kind of binge thinking? If so, please share the thinking binge and, of course, what you (and your child) named it. With your permission, I'd like to post your story and thoughts so other parents can learn from your experiences.

Also, if you need a "Binge Thinking" gift for a high school or college graduate, yourself, your child, or a fellow parent of a college student please visit borgesandwhite.com. Remember, publicizing binge thinking is an important step in curing binge thinking.

In care,
DB

Dear Colleges and Universities,

Are you looking for a program that will prepare students to effectively handle the universal—but often overlooked—phenomenon we call "binge thinking?" Borges and White, LLC provides two educational and entertaining programs for students entitled "How to Cure Binge Thinking."

- · On-site workshops that include real-world exercises for students' real-life binges. Half-day and full-day options available.
- · Keynote addresses that include question and answer sessions.

Students who participate in either program will acquire a "binge" vocabulary for understanding and talking about how binge thinking confronts and conflicts them in and out of the classroom.

We know you care about the well-being of your students. For this reason, a special training seminar for student-life personnel is now being offered to help your staff learn how to diagnose and treat the thinking binges all students endure during their college experience. For bulk book orders, speaking and seminar fees, visit borgesandwhite.com.

In care,
Gino Borges, Ph.D. Zachary White, Ph.D.

About *Borges and White, LLC*

Our high-powered publicist encouraged us to distinguish ourselves by revealing our storied institutional successes—young Ph.D.s, media stars, national speakers, blah, blah, blah…. "Nobody will listen to you unless you reveal your accomplishments. You're experts!" our publicist said. Since she was trained by powerful PR firms, we gave her recommendations the benefit of the doubt. Sooner than later, however, it was clear her advice didn't fit our uncommon sensibilities.

But her advice did turn out to be a blessing because it forced Zachary and me to focus on what we do best (and, of course, what you enjoy most about us). We share our stories and insights not for the purpose of gloating—"I know what's best for you since I'm an expert," but to help you see what occurs in the shadows of achievement and success.

By reading this book, you've indicated that you're into our unconventional logic, which sheds light on the unquestioned aspects of American culture (we like this about ourselves, too). Besides a cup of coffee, tickling American culture so that you can laugh long enough to think—and think long enough to laugh—is what gets us up early in the morning and keeps us going throughout the day.

If you're wondering what happened to the publicist, rest assured: we gave her a raise. Gino and I discovered that to maintain our unique perspective on American culture, we should always have an institutional mouthpiece on staff. She's great. We take what she says and think otherwise. That unbeaten path makes all the difference. If you'd like to help us keep the lights on at Borges and White headquarters, please visit borgesandwhite.com for insights and products and services, including speaking and seminar fees.

978-0-595-34761-2
0-595-34761-4

Printed in the United States
32126LVS00007B/1-102